Classic
E.W. Bullinger
Sermons
A Collection of 14 Sermons

BY E.W. Bullinger

Classic E.W. Bullinger Sermons

A Collection of 14 Sermons

BY E.W. Bullinger

ISBN EAN-13 9798671726336

Published by Alacrity Press, 2020
All rights reserved.
www.alacritypress.com

This book is a product of its time. Some of the terms and views expressed by the author may reflect common values and usage of his day that are contrary to modern values. They should be viewed in that context.

ALACRITY PRESS

Contents

The Three Spheres of Future Glory 1

Christ In The Separate Books Of The Word 9

Stablished — Strengthened — Settled 15

The Rich Man and Lazarus: An Intermediate
    State? Luke 16:19-31 20

Crucified with Christ 51

"Abraham Believed God" 57

The Scope of a Passage May Best Be Discovered
    by Its Structure 62

Right Division 86

The Christian's Greatest Need 91

They Sang His Praise. They Soon Forgat
    His Works 100

The One Great Subject of the Word 105

A New Creation 108

"THE RESURRECTION OF THE BODY" 113

A Refreshing Study On The Resurrection 124

E.W. Bullinger

THE FOUNDATIONS OF DISPENSATIONAL TRUTH
The Three Spheres of Future Glory

THERE is still something more to learn concerning the dispensations before we can rightly understand the unique position and
wonderful teaching of the later Pauline Epistles written from the
prison in Rome. These dispensations are commonly spoken of as: two,
the old and the new, but we must bring them, as all else, to the bar of the
written Word to see whether we have learned from man. or from God,
from tradition or from revelation.

To some extent we shall all agree.

1. We shall all be agreed that the great subject of the Old Testament prophecies is a restored Israel and a re-generated earth (Matt. 19.28).

It is surely unnecessary to quote the many prophecies which tell of
the time when the earth shall be full of the knowledge and glory of the
Lord as the waters cover the sea (Num. 14:21,. Ps. 72:9, Isa. 6:3; 11:9,.
Hab. 2:14).

We are at one with all our readers in taking these prophecies in their
literal meaning; and in not attempting to explain them, or rather fritter
them away by any spiritualizing interpretation which deprives them of
all their truth and power.

We all look forward also to the time when "He that scattered Israel
will gather him" (Jer. 31:10).; when they "shall all be taught of God"
(John 6:45, Isa. 51:13); when "the kingdoms of this world shall become the kingdom of our LORD, and of His Christ" (Rev. 11:15);
and when the earthly Jerusalem shall be restored in more than all its
ancient glory.

That kingdom and sphere of blessing and glory will be on the EARTH;
and the new Israel with a heart of stone changed to a heart of flesh and
with a new spirit, will bring forth "the fruits of righteousness" (Ezek.
36.21-36, Matt. 21:23). This will be the regeneration (or Palingenesia)
when the apostles will be seated "on twelve thrones judging the tribes of
Israel" (Matt. 19. 28). This will be the first and lowest sphere of blessing.
I twill be on EARTH, and under the whole heaven. These are the people
of the saints of the Most High" Dan. 7:27)

All the nations of the earth will share in this blessing according to
God's original promise to Abraham.

2. But Abraham and his spiritual seed are "the saints of the Most High "as distinct from "the people" (of these saints) on the earth (Dan. 7:18, 22, 25), and occupying a distinct place in the HEAVENLY SPHERE of this same kingdom.

These, according to the Lord's words in Luke, are "equal to the angels," "sons of the resurrection" (Luke 20:34 -36) raised in the "first resurrection" before the thousand years of earthly blessing for Israel and for the nations "under the whole heaven" (Deut. 4:19, Rev. 20:4-6). These belong to "that great city the holy Jerusalem," which John saw "descending down from heaven, having the glory of God; and her light like unto a stone most precious." This "holy Jerusalem" is fully described in Rev. 21:9-27. It is the "city which hath THE foundations" for which Abraham had been taught to look (Heb. 11:10) when he "saw Christ's day and was glad" (John 8:56): for, as "faith cometh by hearing," Abraham must have heard: and this "hearing" must have come "from the spoken word of God" (Rom. 10:17).

This is the "inheritance" of those who, as Peter declares to the believers of the Dispersion, "have obtained like precious faith with us." That inheritance" is "incorruptible, and undefiled, and fadeth not away, reserved in HEAVEN for you." The Greek, by the figure Homoioteleutos, emphasizes this "inheritance "as being not earthly, but *aphtharton, amianton, amaranton* (1 Pet. 1:4).

The inhabitants of that heavenly city are declared to be "the bride, the. Lamb's wife" (Rev. 21:9).

From the call of Abraham there have ever been these two seeds, the earthly and the heavenly.

The one was likened by Jehovah to "the dust of the earth" or "the sand of the sea" (Gen. 13. 16; 22. 17); and the other was likened to "the stars of heaven" (Heb. 11:12; Gen. 15:5).

Both expressions suggest multitude, but the former is specially associated with earthly blessing, while the latter points to "the partakers of a heavenly calling (Heb. 3:1).

These latter, like their father Abraham, looked for a heavenly portion and a heavenly blessing, for the city "which hath the foundations."

"These all died in. faith, not having received the promises, but having seen them and greeted them from afar, and having confessed that they were strangers and pilgrims on the earth. For they that say such things make it manifest that they are seeking after a country of their own. And if indeed they had been mindful of that country from which they came out, they would have had opportunity to return. But now they desire a better country, that is a HEAVENLY; wherefore God is not ashamed of them to be called their God; for He hath prepared for them a city" (Heb. 11:13-16, R.V.) Where, and what could that city lave been if it was not the city which John was shown "descending out of heaven from God," the foundations of which are specially described in Rev. 21:19 20.

All through the ages, from Abraham's day to the present, these "partakers of a heavenly calling" may be traced. They formed the congregation of the Lord," and are continually spoken of as such.

Not all Israel, were Tabernacle and Temple frequenters and worshippers. Not all carried out the laws given by Moses, or offered the prescribed sacrifices, attended "the feasts of Jehovah," or carried out the ordered ritual.

Those (probably the few, as we see it to-day) who gathered to the stated worship of Jehovah are called the "assembly" or the "congregation."

The Hebrew word for "congregation "is from kahal (from which doubtless we have our English word "call"). The verb means to call, assemble, gather together: and the noun is used of any assembly thus called. Seventy times in the Septuagint version of the Old Testament it is rendered *ekklesia* (the word for "church" in the New Testament).[1]

It is actually used in the expression the *ekklesia* (or church) of the LORD "in Deut. 23:1, 2, 3, 8, 1 Chron. 28:8 Micah 2:5. In Neh. 13. 1 it is ` the *ekklesia* (or church) of God."

It is this *ekklesia* (or "church") that is referred to as "the congregation" in Ps. 22:22; 26:12; 35:18; 40:9, 10; 68:26.

This is what David means in Psalm 22:22, when he says: "In the midst of the congregation will I praise Thee" (v. 22), and "My praise shall be of Thee in the great congregation " (v. 25.) This is the usage of the same word in the Gospels when the Lord said "Upon this rock will I build My *ekklesia*" (Matt.16:1 8).

He did not, when addressing Israelites, use the word in the new, exclusive and special sense in which it was afterward to be used in the revelation of "the secret" in the Prison Epistles;but in the larger and wider Old Testament sense which His hearers would understand as embracing the whole assembly of Jehovah's believing and worshipping people who were "partakers of a heavenly calling" (Heb. 3:).

When the Spirit by Stephen speaks of "the *ekklesia*" in the wilderness (Acts 7. 38) He means this congregation of pious worshippers.

---

1. In Ps. 22:25 it is spoken of as "the great *ekklesia* or *congregation*," and in Ps. 149:1 as "the *ekklesia* of the saints."

Those who were kept secure under the shadow of the Almighty during the 38 years of penal wanderings in the Wilderness, see Ps. 90 and 91.

When the Lord added to the ekklesia such as were being saved (Acts 2.:47) after Pentecost, He added them to the 120 who before Pentecost assemble (together in the upper room, and who "continued daily in the Temple (no longer offering sacrifices and partaking of the food furnishes thereby), but , breaking bread (or eating; as in Luke 24:30, 35 and Acts 27:35) at home, with gladness and singleness of heart, praising God, and having favour with all the people. "And the Lord added to the church (*ekklesia*) daily such as were being saved " (Acts 2. 46, 47).

It is true that the words "the church" (Gr. *ekklesia*) in vs. 47, are omitted by all the Textual Critics (even the most conservative and least "modern") Lachmann, Tischendorf, Tregelles, Alford, Westcott and Hort, and the Revised version; but we lay no stress on the omission here, because even as it stands, it is used in the Old Testament sense of "the congregation of the LORD," and not in the later sense as found in the Epistle to the Ephesians: for, they would not have understood it (neither should we to-day, if we had never seen that later Epistle).

When Paul says he "persecuted the *ekklesia* of God" (1 Cor. 15:9: Gal. 1:13), he does not use the word in a sense which he had at that time never heard of, or had even the remotest idea of. His words must be understood in the same sense in which he then used them; and we must not read into any passage of Scripture that which was the subject of a subsequent revelation; especially, when the sense is perfectly plain and clear as it stands.

The word *ekklesia* in the Gospels, Acts and the earlier Pauline Epistles must be taken by us in the sense of its Old Testament (Septuagint) usage as meaning simply the congregation or assembly, or company of Jehovah's worshipping people, "partakers of a heavenly calling," having a heavenly hope, a heavenly sphere of blessing, and looking for their part in the "resurrection unto life."

It had been revealed of old that there would be a resurrection, (see Job. 19. 25-27; Hosea 13:14; John 11:24); but it was subsequently revealed also that there would be two resurrections, one to life, and one to judgement. Paul testified of the former as being the hope of those who were worshippers of God (Acts 24:14, 15; David hoped for it (Psalm 16:9-11; 49:14, 15). So did Daniel (Dan. 12. 1-3).

The Lord plainly spoke of the former as "the resurrection of the just" (Luke 14:14); and, as "the resurrection of life " (John 5:29). "By the word of the Lord" was revealed a further hope, or rather, an expression of the hope in John 11:25, 26.

There was not only the hope for those who should have part in the "first resurrection," but for those who should be "alive and remain" when that event should take place.

The "word of the Lord" first mentioned it, and the Holy Spirit by Paul expands it in 1 Thess. 4:16, 17. It concerns the Lord, not only as to His being "the Resurrection," but as to His being "the Life" also. He says:

c | I am the Resurrection
  d | I and the life.
c | He that believeth in Me, though he die, he shall live (again). [To him] I will be "the resurrection "
  d | and everyone who is alive, and believing in Me shall to nowise die, for ever. To him I will be the "Life."

This was (and still is) the hope for all who are "partakers of a heavenly calling" (Heb. 3:1). Many of these were to be found when Messiah came. They were those who waited for the consolation of Israel (Luke 2:25)

who "looked for redemption in Jerusalem" (Luke 2:38),

who "trusted that the Lord was He who should have redeemed Israel" (Luke 24:21),

who "waited for the kingdom of God" (Mark 15:43,; Luke 23:51),

who were "as many as received Him" (John 1:12),

who gladly received Peter's or Paul's word "on the day of Pentecost and after (Acts 2:41, 8:14, 11:1, 17:11),

who received the word in much affliction" (1 Thess. 1:6), and.

who "when they received the word, accepted it not as man's word, but even as it is truly God's word which worketh effectually in you that believe" (1 Thess. 2:13).

who "received not what was promised," (Heb. 11:39) but who believed and embraced it by faith.

Which of us has not been in difficulties as to those we speak of as "the Old Testament saints"?

Well, here they are seen all through the Old Testament as being "the church or assembly of God," "partakers of a heavenly calling," possessing a heavenly hope, and looking for a heavenly sphere of blessing.

3. This brings us to the third sphere, which is the greatest blessing of all, and the highest in glory.

It had been kept secret "from ages and from generations." It is the eternal "purpose" of God, made "before the foundation of the world," and was not "made manifest" by being committed to prophetic writings.

It was a secret not relating to Israel on the earth; nor to the "partakers of a heavenly calling"; but to Christ and the elect members of His body.

Even in the ministry of Christ it was among the things He could not then reveal even to the twelve apostles in the privacy of the upper room after the last supper. Not only could He not say these things then, but the apostles themselves would not have been able to bare them if He had.

And, if the Lord did not mention these things in the Gospels then, certainly the apostles could not have "confirmed "them in the Acts of the Apostles, afterward.

They were" the things of Christ," *i.e.*, those things which stand in a special relation to Him, the things that relate to the whole of the truth. "the truth" which would not be complete without them.

They were, of necessity, reserved for "the Spirit of truth" to reveal. "HE will guide you into the whole of the truth." These precious "riches of grace," and of glory these were the doctrines which had for their foundation the facts of Christ's mission, which had not at that time taken place: though they were all then near at hand.

Those events in Christ's life on earth were the foundation of the doctrines built upon them; and without them the doctrines could not have been known. Until He had suffered, died. risen. and ascended, how could the doctrines of Eph. 2:5, 6 based on them be revealed and taught.

But this special coming, ministry and guidance of "the Spirit of truth" must be held over for our next Editorial: for we must of necessity include that last phase of what "Jehovah hath spoken" before we commence our consideration of the Prison Epistles: for therein and only therein, do we find the "riches" of grace and glory into which the Holy Spirit was to guide: them, the good news of which was destined to fill the long era of Israel's blindness and the nation's dark (spiritual,) night (Isa. 60:1-3).

The Prison Epistles, following immediately after the proclamation of Israel's judicial blindness and hardening (recorded in Acts 28:25, 26), have for their one great subject the revelation of the third of the three spheres of blessing and glory which stands in special relation to Christ and His church.

This sphere is not on the earth.
It is not over the earth.
It is in the highest heavens.

Hence, it has nothing to do with earthly "signs and wonders" that would follow those who in happy obedience believe what is there written.

Such surpassingly exalted language has never before, or since been spoken of human believers.

The very glory of that sphere is inconsistent with any earthly signs or manifestations however wonderful. or, ordinances however once significant.

Those Epistles view the believer of them, not with "signs following," but they view him as "dead" to this world and all earthly associations and connections, and as having jointly suffered, jointly died, jointly risen, and being jointly seated with Christ in the highest heavens.

Even the "affections" and "thoughts" are not to be concerned with the things on earth; they are to be centred on "the things above "where Christ is already seated at the right hand of God. Hence, we do not read in those Epistles about the coming of Christ to the earth, but rather about our being removed to be with Him where pie is, not about His parousia, or presence on earth, or "in the air"; but about our presence and manifestation with Him in His own glory; not about anastasis or resurrection (which is the subject of the earlier Pauline Epistles), but about an "*ex-anastasis*," (Phil. 3:11) and "the calling on high" (Phil. 3:14) which is the subject of the later Epistles; not about any personal happiness which we may have, but about Christ's personal glory, in which we have the wondrous privilege of sharing.

In this connection we would call attention to one word, which, in our judgment, is the real keyword of the Prison Epistles, and of this third and highest sphere. It is a remarkable word, found. in this form, only here, in the New Testament. It occurs once before in Rom. 13:9, but there it is in the present passive voice (*anakephalaioutai*), and means "is summed up." But in Eph. 1:10 it is the Aorist Infinitive of the middle voice, (*anakephalaiosasthai*). This difference is ignored both by the Authorised and the Revised Versions, which read the middle voice of Eph. 1. to as though it were the Active. This is an almost unpardonable oversight, in the interest of the ordinary Bible reader, who has an undoubted right to a correct grammatical rendering from such a quarter.

Translated correctly, the word and the entire passage emphasize the underlying fact that in all things there revealed, our Heavenly Father has,

FOR HIMSELF, purposed what is here stated, *viz.*, that according to
His good pleasure, which He purposed in Himself, in order to a dispensation of the fullness of the seasons, TO-SUM-UP-FOR-HIMSELF, every thing in Christ: things in heaven and things on earth, even in Him,
in whom we were taken as an inheritance, being foreordained according
to the purpose of Him who worketh all things according to the counsel
of His own will, that we should be to the praise of His glory who have
before hoped in Christ.

This will be enough to show us that the Cosmos, as shown in Col.
1:15, 16, is a larger, higher, and greater sphere than[2] that of earthly glory,
or (a) that of the glory reserved for those who are "partakers of a heavenly calling."

The Old Testament, the Acts and the earlier Pauline Epistles deal with
these two lower spheres of glory, but the later Epistles reveal a third
sphere of Headship and Heirship above the earth or the heavens.

1 Cor. 15:40 tells of "terrestrial "glory and of "celestial's glory, which
differ the one from the other.

But there is a third sphere; a sphere of cosimical glory (if we may
use the word in this connection) high above all created beings, whether
principalities, or powers, or, might, or thrones, or dominions, which are
mentioned (though not defined or explained) in Eph. 1:21, Col. 1:16 in
relation to Christ, who shall be "Head over all."

This includes the putting down of all enemies, and the final crushing
of the head of "the old serpent" the devil.

This is why the enemy's great endeavour, now, is to blind the minds
of men so that the light of this "good news (or gospel) of the glory of
Christ" should be hidden from them" (2 Cor. 4:3, 1).

And this is why we, who obey God by believing Him as to this, His
greatest and most glorious revelation, should cherish it as our earnest
hope and constant theme; and, not being ignorant of Satan's devices,
since we are thus told against what his assault is being made, therefore
know where our defence is to be directed.

In other words, we are to labour to make known: "the riches of glory"
which are connected with this third and Highest sphere of blessing and
glory and honour for "Christ and His Church."

---

2. 1. Though the recent discovery of Radium is beginning to open our eyes and show how
   light can exist without the sun.

Christch In The Separate Books Of The Word

In GENESIS we shall understand the record of Creation (ch. 1), for we shall see in it the counterpart of our new creation in Christ Jesus (II Cor. v. 17). In the light which shined out of darkness (Gen. 1:2, 3) we shall see the light which has shone "in our hearts to give the knowledge of the glory of God in the face (or person) of Jesus Christ" (II Cor. 4:6). No wonder that those who know nothing of this spiritual light of the New Creation know nothing of the light that was created on the first day as revealed in the record of the old creation.

The natural man sees only a myth and an old wives' fable in the Creation record, and seems actually to prefer the Babylonian corruption of primitive truth. These "other Gentiles walk in the vanity of their mind, having the understanding darkened, being alienated from the life of God through the ignorance that is in them, because of the blindness of their heart" (Eph. iv. 17,18). Woe be to those who follow these blind leaders, for "they shall both fall into the ditch" they have prepared for themselves by their fleshly knowledge and worldly wisdom. In the Creator we shall see Christ (John 1:3. Col. 1:16).

In the first Adam we shall see the last Adam (I Cor. 15:45. Rom. 5:14). In the first man we shall see "the second man, the Lord, from heaven" (I Cor. 15:47).

In the "seed of the woman" (Gen. 3:15) we shall see the coming son of Abraham, the son of David, the Son of man, the Son of God; while those who are in the black darkness of Rome see either a helpless Infant, or a dead man, and a living woman—the Virgin Mary; having corrupted their Authorized Vulgate Version (in Gen. 3:15), to make it the foundation of this blasphemy. [3]

In Abraham's shield we shall see the Living Word, coming, speaking, and revealing Himself to him (ch. 15:1. John 8:56).

In Isaac we shall see Christ the true seed of Abraham (Rom. 9:7. Gal. 3:16).

In the Annunciation to the Mother (Gen. 18:10. Luke 1:30-33), the miraculous conception (Gen. 18:14. Luke 1:35) and the pre-natal naming (Gen. 17:19. Matt. 1:21. Luke 1:31; 2:21).

In the projected death of the one we see the foreshadowing of the other, two thousand years before, and on the same mountain, Moriah; and this Mount, selected not by chance, or for convenience

---

3. Where the Hebrew masculine is misrepresented as feminine, and is thus made, as Dr. Pusey has said, the foundation of Mariolatry, and the basis of the Immaculate Conception.

(for it was three days journey), but appointed in the Divine counsels as the site of the future altar of burnt offering (Gen. 22:2. I Chron. 21:28-22:1. 2 Chron. 3:1).

In the wood laid upon Isaac (Gen. 22:6), and not carried by the servants or on the ass, we shall see Him who was led forth bearing His Cross (John 19:17).

In Joseph, of whom the question was asked, "Shalt thou indeed reign over us?" we see Him of whom His brethren afterwards said, "We will not have this man to reign over us" (Luke 19:14). But we see the sufferings of the one followed by the glory, as we shall surely see the glory of the true Joseph following His sufferings in the fulness of time (1 Pet. 1:11), of which glory we shall be the witnesses, and partakers (1 Pet. 4:13; v. 1).

We must not pursue this great subject or principle in its further details, though we have but touched the fringe of it, even in the book of Genesis. As the Lord Jesus began at Moses so have we only made a beginning, and must leave our readers to follow where we have pointed out the way.

It may be well, however, for us to indicate one or two of the leading points of the other books of the Old Testament.

EXODUS tells of the sufferings and the glory of Moses, as Genesis does of Joseph, and in both we see a type of the sufferings and glory of Christ.

Joseph's sufferings began with his rejection, his own brethren asking, "Shalt thou indeed reign over us? Or shalt thou indeed have dominion over us?" (Gen. 37:8). Moses' sufferings began with his rejection and the question of "two men of the Hebrews,"—"Who made thee a ruler and a judge over us?" (Exod. 2:14). In all this we see the rejection of Christ by a similar question, the thought of their hearts being put into their lips, in the parable, where "his citizens hated Him and sent a message after Him saying, 'We will not have this man to reign over us'" (Luke 19:11).

But the issue in all three cases is the same. Of each it is true, as it is said of Moses, "This Moses whom they refused, saying, 'Who made thee a ruler and a deliverer?' The same did God send to be a ruler and a judge by the hand of the angel which appeared to him in the bush" (Acts 7:35). Even so will God surely "send Jesus Christ whom the heavens must receive until the times of restitution of all things which God hath spoken by the mouth of all His holy prophets since the world began" (Acts 3:20, 21).

Thus early, in Genesis and Exodus, we have the great subject of the sufferings and the glory of Christ more than foreshadowed (1 Pet. 1:11; 4:13; 5:1. Luke 24:26). Exodus tells us also of Christ as the true Paschal Lamb (I Cor. v. 7, 8); as the true Priest (Exod. 30:10. Heb. 5:4, 5); and the true Tabernacle which the Lord pitched and not men (Heb. 9).

LEVITICUS gives us, in the offerings, a fourfold view of the Death of Christ (the Sin and Trespass Offerings being reckoned as one), as the Gospels give us a fourfold view of His life. NUMBERS foreshadows the Son of Man come to be lifted up" (ch. 21:9. John 3:14, 15); the Rock (ch. 20:11. I Cor. 10:4); the Manna that fed them (ch. 11:7-9. Deut. 8:2, 3. John 6:57, 58); and the future Star that should arise "out of Jacob" (ch. 24:17. Luke 1:78. II Pet. 1:19. Rev. 2:28; 22:16).

DEUTERONOMY reveals the coining Prophet "like unto Moses" (ch. 18:15. Acts 7: 23- 26); the Rock and Refuge of His people (chs. 22:4; 23:27).

JOSHUA tells of "the Captain of the Lord's host" (ch. 5:13-15. Heb. 2:10; 12:2) who shall triumph over all His foes; while Rahab's scarlet cord (ch. 2:12-20) tells of His sufferings and precious blood which will shelter and preserve His people in the coming day of His war.

JUDGES tells of the Covenant Angel whose name is "Secret," i.e. "Wonderful" (ch. 13:18, margin; compare Isa. 9:6, where the word is the same).

RUTH reveals the type of our Kinsman-Redeemer, the true Boaz; and the question of ch. 2:10 is answered in Prov. 11:15.

SAMUEL reveals the "sufferings" and rejection of David, who became a "Saviour" and a "Captain" of his followers (I Sam. 22:1, 2), foreshadowing David's Son and David's Lord, "the Root and the Offspring of David" (Rev. 22:16).

KINGS shows us the "glory which should follow," and the "greater than Solomon" (Matt. 12:42); the "greater than the Temple" (Matt. 12:6), where everything speaks of His glory (Ps. 29:9 and margin).

CHRONICLES reveals Christ as "the King's Son," rescued "from among the dead," hidden in the House of God, to be manifested in due time, "as Jehovah hath said" (II Chron. 22:10–23:3).

EZRA speaks of "a nail in a sure place" (ch. 9:8), which according to Isa. 22:23 is used of Eliakim, who typifies Christ.

NEHEMIAH tells of the "bread from Heaven" and "water out of the Rock" (ch. 9:15, 20), which are elsewhere used as typical of Christ (John 6:57, 58. I Cor. 10:4).

ESTHER sees the seed preserved which should in the fulness of time be born into the world. His name is there, though concealed, but His will and power is manifested in defeating all enemies in spite of the un-alterable law of the Medes and Persians. [4]

JOB reveals Him as his "Daysman" or "Mediator" (ch. 9:33); and as his "Redeemer" coming again to the earth (ch. 19:25-27).

THE PSALMS are full of Christ. We see His humiliation and sufferings and death (Ps. 22), His Resurrection (Ps. 16), His anointing as Prophet with grace-filled lips (Ps. 55, Luke 4:22); as Priest after the order of Melchizedek (Ps. 110, Heb. 5:6; 6:20; 7:17, 21); as King enthroned over all (Ps. 2), and His kingdom established in the earth (Ps. 103.; 145, & 100).

PROVERBS reveals Christ as the "Wisdom of God" (ch. 8, I Cor. 1:24); the "Path" and "Light" of His People (ch. 4:18); the "Surety" who smarted for His people while strangers (ch. 11:15. Rom. 5:8-10. Eph. 2:12.[5] Pet. 2:11); the "strong tower" into which the righteous run and are safe (ch. 18:10); the friend who loveth at all times, and the brother born for adversity (ch. 17:17).

ECCLESIASTES tells of the "one among a thousand in the midst of all that is vanity and vexation of spirit" (ch. 7:28).

---

4. See *The Name of Jehovah in the Book of Esther, in Four Acrostics,* by the same author.
5. Though the recent discovery of Radium is beginning to open our eyes and show how light can exist without the sun.

THE SONG OF SONGS reveals Him as the true and faithful Shepherd, Lover, and Bridegroom of the Bride, who remained constant to Him in spite of all the royal grandeur and coarser blandishments of Solomon.

ISAIAH is full of the sufferings and glories of Christ. He is the "despised and rejected of men, a man of sorrows, and acquainted with grief" (ch. 53:5); wounded for our transgressions, oppressed, afflicted, and brought as a lamb to the slaughter; cut off out of the land of the living (ch. 53:2–9). Yet the glory shall follow. "He shall see of the travail of His soul and be satisfied" (ch. 53:11). He will be His people's "Light" (ch. 60:1, 2. Matt. 4:16); "The Mighty God" (ch. 9:6. Matt. 28:18); Salvation's Well (ch. 12:3); the King who shall "reign in righteousness" (ch. 22:1, 2); Jehovah's Branch, beautiful and glorious (ch. 4:2).

JEREMIAH tells of "the Righteous Branch," and "Jehovah our Righteousness" (ch. 23:5, 6); of the "Righteous Branch" and King who shall reign and prosper (ch. 33:15).

EZEKIEL reveals Him as the true Shepherd (ch. 34:23), and as "the Prince" (ch. 37:25); the "Plant of Renown" (ch. 34:29), and "Jehovah Shammah" (ch. 48:35).

DANIEL reveals Him as the "Stone" become the Head of the corner (ch. 2:34. Ps. 118:22. Isa. 8:14. 28:16. Matt. 21:42, 44. Acts 4. I Pet. 2:4, 6). Also as the Son of Man (ch. 7:13, 16); and "Messiah the Prince" (ch. 9:24).

He is **HOSEA'S** true David (3:5), the Son out of Egypt (11:1); JOEL'S "God dwelling in Zion" (ch. 3:17);

AMOS'S Raiser of David's Tabernacle (ch. 9:11; Acts 15:16, 17);

OBADIAH'S "Deliverer on Mount Zion" (v. 17);

JONAH'S "Salvation" (ch. 2:9); the "Sign" of Christ's resurrection (Matt. 12:39-41);

MICAH'S "Breaker," "King" and "Lord" (ch. 2:13; 5:2,5);

NAHUM'S "Stronghold in Trouble" (ch. 1:7);,

HABAKKUK'S "Joy" and "Confidence" (ch. 3:17, 18);

ZEPHANIAH'S "Mighty God in the midst of Zion" (ch. 3:17);

HAGGAI'S "Desire of all nations" (ch. 2:7);

ZECHARIAH'S Smitten Shepherd; The Man, Jehovah's Fellow (ch. 13:7); Jehovah's "Servant- the Branch" (ch. 3:8); "the Man whose name is the Branch" (ch. 6:12);

MALACHI'S "Messenger of the Covenant" (ch. 3: 1); the Refiner of the Sons of Levi (ch. 3:3); "The Sun of Righteousness" (ch. 4:2). Thus, the "Word" of God has one great subject. That one great all-pervading subject is Christ; and all else stands in relation to Him. He is "the beginning and the ending" of Scripture, as of all beside. Hence, the Word of God, at its ending, shows how the beginning all works out; and how, that to which we are introduced in Genesis is completed in Revelation. Satan's first rebellion is implied between the first and second verses of the first chapter of Genesis, and his final rebellion is seen in Rev. 20:7-9. His doom is pronounced in Gen. 3:15, and is accomplished in Rev. 20:10. We have the primal Creation, "the world that then was," in Gen. 1:1 (II Pet. 3:6). "The Heavens and the Earth which are now" in Gen. 1:2, etc. (2 Pet. 3:7). And "The New Heavens and the New Earth" in Rev. 21:1 (2 Pet. 3:13). We have "night" in Gen. 1:1; and see "no night there" in Rev. 22:5.

We have the "sea" in Gen. 1:10; and "no more sea" in Rev. 21:1. We have the "sun and moon" in Gen. 1:16, 17; and "no need of the sun or the moon" in Rev. 21:23; 22:5. We have the entrance of sorrow and suffering and death in Gen. 3:16, 17; and "no more death, neither sorrow nor crying" in Rev. 21:4. We have the "curse" pronounced in Gen. 3:17; and "no more curse" in Rev. 22:3. We have banishment from Paradise and the Tree of Life in Gen. 3:22-24; and the welcome back and "right to it" in Rev. 22:2. This will be sufficient[6] to show the unity of the "Word" as a whole; and to stimulate Bible students to a further study of it on the line of this great fundamental principle.

---

6. More instances will be found in *The Apocalypse, or, the Day of the Lord*, republished as *Commentary on Revelation*, by Kregel Publications, pp. 58, 59.

Stablished—Strengthened—Settled

The God of all grace who hath called us unto His eternal glory, by Christ Jesus, after that we have suffered awhile, make you perfect. stablish, strengthen, settle you. To Him be glory and dominion for ever and ever. Amen" (I Peter 5:10,11).

These words contain a prayer for a very special blessing. But in order to obtain it we are cast upon the God of all grace—God, who performeth all things for us. Thus we have in this verse four things:

    1. The God of all grace.
    2. His effectual calling.
    3. The necessary suffering.
    4. The certain blessing.

1. The God of all grace

We must not dwell on the first of these (if we are to consider the others), for it is a subject in itself—a vast subject. For we are lost in wonder, love, and praise, the moment we enter upon the consideration of "the God of all grace," and survey His sovereign grace, His redeeming, grace, His saving grace, His justifying grace, His providing grace, His abounding grace, His exceeding grace: and all this uninfluenced grace, invincible grace, inexhaustible and immutable grace.

What grace! All treasured up in Jesus Christ who is "full of grace," and He alone. It can never be said of any mortal as it is said of Mary, "Hail, Mary, full of grace!" in perversion of Luke 1:28, in all the Romish versions. No! all grace is treasured up for us in Christ, and He holds it at His own disposal. Let us pass on to the second point.

2. His effectual calling

"Who hath called us unto His eternal glory," not, who is calling us, not, who may call us, but "who hath called us," a past, completed act, and that not to a temporal glory, nor to a fleeting transient glory, but to a glory which knew no beginning and can know no end. If He has called us, it is to His eternal glory. If He has called us, we shall have experienced our inability to obey. That is why it is here, "The God of all grace."

When God commands, the first thing we do is to discover our inability to obey; it is this which fills us with anxiety to be saved. When He calls, we immediately discover that we are like Mephibosheth in II Samuel 9.

We are at Lo-Debar, a "place of no pasture." We have nothing really to sustain us, we are clothed in filthy garments, we are not worthy to come into the King's presence, not meet to sit at the King's table, and, moreover, "lame on both feet" (verse 13). When King David called Mephibosheth, how could he obey? But David called him not for his own sake. He said, "Is there yet any that is left of the house of Saul that I may shew him kindness for Jonathan's sake?" (verse 1). "Fear not: for I will surely shew thee kindness for Jonathan thy Father's sake" (verse 7). Still, how could he obey, being lame on his feet? We learn in verse 15, only by being sent for, fetched and carried. And so with us. The Lord Himself must be the carrier, the sender, the fetcher, or the appointer of those who shall do so.

Like the man sick of the palsy; he was carried to the Lord Jesus Christ, and it is written, "Jesus seeing their faith." Why is it that we immediately and universally think of the four and not of the five. Why do we exclude the man himself? Had he no faith, no desire? How do we know but that it was he who urged his friends to carry him? It is only our own perversity that thus limits God's grace. Yes, and "When Jesus saw their faith" He saw the desire of His own heart, the work of His own hands. Where there is the Master's gracious call, there will also be His careful carrying.

"Who hath called us unto His eternal glory?" How does He call? By Jesus Christ, it says. Yes, it is all by Christ, with Christ, through Christ, in Christ. Called by Christ to the experience of identification with Him in the glory of God the Father, we are comforted with the fact that as the Head is, so are the members of the body of Christ. .As the Father sees Him, so He sees His members. They are glorified together in the purpose of God. But as Jehovah the Spirit brings them into the apprehension of what they are in Christ, it is then that they discover their corrupt and depraved condition. It is then they cry, "I am black," "I am vile," "I am undone." But the declaration of His grace-filled lips is, "Thou art all fair, my love, there is no spot in thee." That is glory! Can we believe it? Only as He brings this precious truth home to us by the power of the Holy Spirit. It is thus that we, as the members of His body, realize something of the glory we possess in and through Him.

3. The necessary suffering

"After that ye have suffered awhile." Have we been called to His eternal glory? Then we have the call to suffering also. Has Christ left us the legacy of His peace (John 16:33)? He has left us the legacy of tribulation also. Then in the world we shall have tribulation. Do the consolations of Christ abound in us? Then the sufferings also abound (II Corinthians 1:5). But we have this testimony concerning them: "That no man should be moved by these afflictions: for yourselves know that we are appointed thereunto, for, verily, when we were with you, we told you before that we should suffer tribulation, even as it came to pass, and ye know" (I Thessalonians 3:3,4). Is it not a mercy to know this blessed truth, so that we may not be moved? To know that there is not a pain or anxiety or trial or care but what comes in all wisdom, and is accompanied by infinite love.

Have you experienced any of them? What have you done with them? Does your conscience condemn you for having taken them to anyone but to Him, who calls you by them to Himself? May the Lord ever enable us to carry our anxieties, our cares, our distresses and our sorrows to Himself. He alone can comfort us, He alone can deliver us in His own good time. Hence we pray in our service, "We commend to Thy Fatherly goodness all those who are anyways afflicted in mind, body or estate, that it may please Thee to comfort and relieve them according to their several necessities, giving them patience under their sufferings, and a happy issue out of all their afflictions." Our hearts respond to that. There is true fellowship there. "The God of all grace who hath called us unto His eternal glory by Christ Jesus, after that ye have suffered awhile, make you perfect, stablish, strengthen, settle you." Christian sympathy breathed in that prayer.

If we are called to His eternal glory, we shall be called to suffering also. If we are called to experience spiritual union with a risen Christ in the heavenlies, to enjoy fellowship with the Father, Son and Holy Spirit (Ephesians 2:6), we shall also experience conflict with wicked spirits in the same heavenlies (Ephesians 6:12). The very place of favour is the scene of conflict. You see this in the case of the Lord Jesus Himself. "Lo, a voice from heaven saying, 'This is My beloved Son in whom I am well pleased.' Then was Jesus led up of the Spirit into the wilderness to be tempted of the devil." You see the same in His servant Paul (II Corinthians 12:1-10). Paul was in the third heaven, blest with extraordinary revelations of eternal glory, yet there was the necessary suffering, '"a messenger of Satan to buffet him." "A man in Christ," yet a man "buffeted" by an angel of Satan. But after he had suffered awhile he was stablished, strengthened, settled by those gracious words, "My grace is sufficient for thee for My strength is made perfect in weakness." This brings us to...

4. The certain blessing

"Make you perfect." What are we to understand by these words? It is a word of simple meaning, but full of instruction. It means to adjust, put in order again. Among the Greeks it was the technical surgical term for setting a bone, a medical term for making up and preparing medicine. It was also a nautical term for fitting out, refitting or repairing a ship. We have its various meanings, all true in a spiritual sense, expressed in this prayer; it is the prayer for us to pray, and it expresses the work of God for us.

The following are some occurrences of the word, and they illustrate its use: (Matthew 4:21), "He saw other two brethren... with their father mending their nets." (Galatians 6:1). "If a man be overtaken in a fault, ye that are spiritual restore such a one." (Hebrews 10:5), "A body hast Thou prepared (margin fitted) Me." (I Corinthians 1:10), "Perfectly joined together." Who can mend our ways and repair our nets? Restore us when overtaken in a fault, prepare our hearts, join us together in the same mind, the same mind that was in Christ Jesus, but the God of all grace?

It is He also who can stablish us. This speaks of permanency. "It came to pass when the time was come that He should be received up He steadfastly set His face to go to Jerusalem (Luke 9:51); i.e., His purpose was stablished, fixed, settled; nothing could move it. "And the Lord said, 'Simon, Simon, Satan hath desired to have you (plural) that he may sift you (plural) as wheat, but I have prayed for thee that thy faith fail not, and when thou art converted strengthen (i.e., stablish) thy brethren'" (Luke 22:31,32). That is the very thing Peter is doing by the Holy Spirit here in our text. He was obeying by the Spirit this very command. May he by these words stablish us his brethren now.

His very example stablishes us, for though Peter failed and fell, his faith did not fail, it was the faith of the operation of God, and neither men nor demons, neither Peter's sins, Peter's wavering, or Peter's doubting could ever mar the fair beauty of that faith which stood not "in the wisdom of men, but in the power of God" (I Corinthians 2:5). Peter's faith had many a shaking, but it was stablished upon the truth of his God, upon the person and work and righteousness of Jesus Christ. A faith, so stablished by the "God of all grace," reconciles the heart to His mysterious and sometimes perplexing providences, and nothing shall ever remove it from its foundation. Peter does not say that we are to arrive at any state of perfection, or at this stablishing by praying, by believing, or by any act of faith or act of surrender as it is popularly called. No. He looks to the God of all grace to do it all for us. "Strengthen."

Why are those who are stablished in Christ to be strengthened? Because in themselves they are weak and often faint and weary. See how we read of this strengthening in the case of Paul (II Corinthians 12:5-10). Paul had no strength out of Christ, and yet he was "strong in the

Lord, and in the power of His might" (Ephesians 6:10). He could do all things through Christ strengthening Him (Philippians 4:13). He was "strengthened with all might according to His glorious power unto all patience and long-suffering with joyfulness" (Colossians 1:11). God, having commanded strength for His people, secures it to them in the Son of His love, and performs it in them by His Spirit. Therefore this is their supplication. "Strengthen, O God, that which Thou hast wrought for us" (Psalm 68:28). "Settled." Settled means grounded, founded as on a foundation. What mercy to be grounded and settled in the faith so as not to be "moved away from the hope of the gospel" (Colossians 1:23). It is a great blessing to be on God's sure foundation, but it is a greater blessing to be settled thereon. If we know anything of this spiritual settling upon the one foundation which God has laid in Christ, that settling will be experienced in connection with suffering, stablishing, and strengthening.

Those who are by the God of all grace called unto His eternal glory, and are suffering for a little while in fellowship with a despised and rejected Lord, who are perfect only in Christ, those whom He is stablishing, strengthening and settling in the faith, the fear, the truth of God, will be able to sing the glorious doxology .of I Peter 5:11, "To Him be glory and dominion for ever and ever. Amen."

The Rich Man and Lazarus:
An Intermediate State?
Luke 16:19-31

In dealing with this Scripture, and the subject of the so-called "intermediate state", it is important that we should confine ourselves to the Word of God, and not go to Tradition. Yet, when nine out of ten believe what they have learned from Tradition, we have a thankless task, so far as pleasing man is concerned. We might give our own ideas as the the employment's, etc., of the "departed," and man would deal leniently with us. But let us only put God's Revelation against man's imagination, and then we shall be made to feel his wrath, and experience his opposition.

Claiming, however, to have as great a love and jealousy for the Word of God as any of our brethren; and as sincere a desire to find out what God says, and what God means: we claim also the sympathy of all our fellow members of the Body of Christ. There are several matters to be considered before we can reach the Scripture concerning the rich man and Lazarus; or arrive at a satisfactory conclusion as to the State after death. It will be well for us to remember that all such expressions as "Intermediate State," "Church Triumphant," and others similar to them are unknown to Scripture. They have been inherited by us from Tradition, and have been accepted without thought or examination.

Putting aside, therefore, all that we have thus been taught, let us see what God actually does reveal to us in Scripture concerning man, in life, and in death; and concerning the state and condition of the dead.

Psalm 146:4 declared of man,

> *"His breath goeth forth, He returneth to his earth; In that very day his thoughts perish."*

God is here speaking of "Man"; not of some part of man, but of "princes," and "man" or any "son of man" (v. 3), *i.e.* Any and every human being begotten or born of human parents. There is not a word about "disembodied man." No such expression is to be found in the Scriptures! The phrase is man's own invention in order to make this and other scriptures agree with his tradition. This Scripture speaks of "man" as man. "His breath"; "he returneth"; "his thoughts." It is an unwarrantable liberty to put "body" when the Holy Spirit has put "man."

The passage says nothing about the "body." It is whatever has done this thinking. The "body" does not think. The "body" apart from the spirit has no "thoughts." Whatever has had the "thoughts" has them no more; and this is "man." If this were the only statement in Scripture on the subject it would be sufficient. But there are many others.

There is Ecc. 9:5, which declares that "The dead know not anything." This also is so clear that there could be no second meaning. "The dead" are the dead; they are those who have ceased to live; and, if the dead do or can know anything, then words are useless for the purpose of revelation. The word "dead" here is used in the immediate context as the opposite of "the living," *e.g.*:

> *"The living know that they shall die, But the dead know not anything"*

It does not say dead bodies know not anything, but "the dead," *i.e.* dead people, who are set in contrast with "the living." As one of these "living" David says, by the Holy Spirit (Psalm 146:2)

> *"While I live will I praise the Lord: I will sing praises unto my God while I have any being."*

There would be no praising after he ceased to "live." Nor would there be any singing of praises after he had cease to "have any being." Why? Because "princes" and "the son of man" are helpless (Psalm 146:3,4). They return to their earth; and when they die, their "thoughts perish": and they "know not anything."

This is what God says about death. He explains it to us Himself. We need not therefore ask any man what it is. And if we did, his answer would be valueless, inasmuch as it is absolutely impossible for him to know anything of death, *i.e.* the death-state, as we have no noun in English to express the act of dying (as German has in the word "sterbend"). This is unfortunate, and has been the cause of much error and confusion.

We find the answer is just as clear and decisive in Psalm 104:29,30:

> *"Thou takest away their breath (Heb. spirit), they die,*
> *And return to their dust:*
> *Thou sendest forth thy spirit, they are created:*
> *And thou renewest the face of the earth."*

With this agrees Ecc. 12:7, in which we have a categorical statement as to what takes place at death:

"Then shall the dust RE-turn to the earth as it was: And the spirit shall RE-turn unto God who gave it".

The "dust" was, and will again be "dust": but nothing is said in Scripture as to the spirit apart from the body, either before their union, which made man "a living soul," or after that union is broken, when man becomes what Scripture calls "a dead soul."

Where Scripture is silent, we may well be silent too: and, therefore, as to the spirit and its possibilities between dying and resurrection we have not said, and do not say, anything. Scripture says it will "return to GOD." We do not go beyond this; nor dare we contradict it by saying, with Tradition, that it goes to Purgatory or to Paradise; or with Spiritualism, that it goes elsewhere.

The prayer in I Thess. 5:23 is that these three (body, soul, and spirit) may be found and "preserved ENTIRE...at the coming of our Lord Jesus Christ" (R.V.): i.e. preserved alive as a "living soul" till (or "at") that coming; and not to die and be separated before it. Hence the importance of Resurrection as the great doctrine peculiar to Christianity; and known only by revelation. All man's religions end at death, and his only hope is "after death." Christianity goes beyond this, and gives a hope after the grave. Scripture shuts us up to the blessed hope of being reunited in resurrection. This is why the death of believers is so often called "sleep"; and dying is called "falling asleep"; because of the assured hope of awaking in resurrection. It is not called "the sleep of the body" as many express it; or "the sleep of the soul." Scripture knows nothing of either expression. Its language is, "David fell on sleep" (Acts 13:36), not David's body or David's soul. "Stephen...fell asleep" (Acts 7:60). "Lazarus sleepeth" (John 11:11), which is explained, when the Lord afterward speaks "plainly," as meaning "Lazarus is dead" (v. 14).

Now, when the Holy Spirit uses one thing to describe or explain another, He does not choose the opposite word or expression. If He speaks of night, He does not use the word light. If He speaks of daylight, He does not use the word night. He does not put "sweet for bitter, and bitter for sweet" (Isa. 5:20). He uses adultery to illustrate Idolatry; He does not use virtue. And so, if He uses the word "sleep" of death, it is because sleep illustrates to us what the condition of death is like. If Tradition be the truth, He ought to have used the word awake, or wakefulness. But the Lord first uses a Figure, and says "Lazarus sleepeth"; and afterwards, when he speaks "plainly" He says "Lazarus is dead." Why? Because sleep expresses and describes the condition of the "unclothed" state. In normal sleep, there is no consciousness. For the Lord, therefore, to have used this word "sleep" to represent the very opposite condition of conscious wakefulness, would have been indeed to mislead us. But all His words are perfect; and are used for the purpose of teaching us, and not for leading us astray.

Traditionalists, however, who say that death means life, do not hesitate to say also that to "fall asleep" means to wake up! A friend vouches for a case, personally known to him, of one who (though a firm believer in tradition) was, through a fall, utterly unconscious for two weeks. Had he died during that period,

Traditionalists would, we presume, say that the man woke up and returned to consciousness when he died! But, if this be so, what does it mean when it says,

> *"I will behold thy face in righteousness: I shall be satisfied, when I Awake with thy likeness"?*

If death is waking up, what is the waking in this verse (Psalm 17:15)? Surely it is resurrection, which is the very opposite of falling asleep in death. Indeed, this is why sleep is used of the Lord's people. To them it is like going to sleep; for when they are raised from the dead they will surely wake again according to the promise of the Lord; and they shall awake in His own likeness.

And if we ask what life is, the answer from God is given in Gen. 2:7:

> *"The Lord God formed man of the dust of the ground, And breathed into his nostrils the breath of life, And man became a living soul."*

So that the body apart from the spirit cannot be the man; and the spirit apart from the body is not the man; but it is the union of the two that makes "a living soul." When two separate things, having different names, are united, they often receive and are known by a third name, different from both. Not that they are three separate beings, but two united in one, which makes a third tiling, and receives another or third name. For example, there is the barrel, and there is the stock; but, together, they form and are called a Rifle. Neither is the Rifle separately. Oxygen and Hydrogen are two separate and distinct elements; but when they are united, we call them Water. So also we have the case, and the works; but together they form what we call a Watch; neither is the Watch separately.

The Hebrew is *Nephesh Chaiyah,* soul of life, or living soul. What it really means can be known only by observing how the Holy Spirit Himself uses it. In this very chapter (Gen. 2:19) it is used of the whole animate creation generally; and is rendered "living creature."

Four times it is used in the previous chapter (Gen. 1.): In verse 20 it is used of "fishes," and is translated "moving creature that hath life." In verse 21 it is used of the great sea monsters, and is translated "living creature." In verse 24 it is used of "cattle and beasts of the earth," and is again rendered "living creature." In verse 30 it is used of "every beast of the earth, and every fowl of the air, and every living thing that creepeth upon the earth wherein there is (*i.e.* "to" which there is) life. Margin "Heb. living soul."

Four times in chapter 9 it is also rendered "living creature," and is used of "all flesh." See verses 10, 12, 15, 16.

Twice in Leviticus 11 it is used: In verse 10 of all fishes, and is rendered "living thing." In verse 46 of all beasts, birds, and fishes, and is translated "living creature."

Only once (Gen. 2:7) when it is used of man, has it been translated "living soul"—as though it there meant something quite different altogether.

The Translators could accurately have used one rendering for all these passages, and thus enabled Bible students to learn what God teaches on this important subject.

This then is God's answer to our question, What is life? The teaching of Scripture is (as we have seen) that man consists of two parts: body and spirit; and that the union of these two makes a third thing, which is called "soul" or "living soul." Hence the word "soul" is used of the whole personality; the living 'organism' e.g. Gen. 12:5, "Abram took Sarai his wife...and the souls (*i.e.* the persons) whom they had gotten in Haran." Gen 36:6, "And Esau took his wives...and all the persons (marg. Heb. souls) of his house." So 46:15, and 26, "All the souls (*i.e.* persons) which came with Jacob into Egypt." As persons, souls have "blood" Jer. 2:34, "In thy skirts is found the blood of the souls of the poor innocents." The Hebrew word nephesh (soul) is actually translated "person" in Gen. 14:21; 36:6. Ex. 16:16. Lev. 27:2. Num. 5:6; 31:19; 35:11, 15, 30 (twice). Deut. 10:22; 27:25. Josh. 20:3, 9. I Sam. 22:22. Sam. 14:14. Prov. 28:17. Jer. 43:6; 52:29, 30. Ezek. 16:5; 17:17; 27:13; 33:6.

Hence, the Lord Jesus says, "Fear not them which kill the body, but are not able to kill the soul (*i.e.* the 'personality') but rather fear him which is able to destroy both soul and body (*i.e.* the whole personality) in hell" (Greek, *Gehenna,* not *Hades*) (Matt. 10:28).

Hence, souls (as persons) are said to be destroyed: Lev. 5:1, 2, 4, 15, 17; 6:2; 17:11, 12. Num. 15:30. See also Joshua 10:20, 30, 32, 35, 37, 39.

The soul, being the person, is said to be bought and sold. See Lev. 22:11, and Rev. 18:13, where the word "soul" is used of slaves.

Hence, also, when the body returns to dust and the spirit returns to God, the person is called a "dead soul," *i.e.* a dead person. That is why it says in Ezek. 18:4, "The soul that sinneth, it shall die"; and Psalm 78:50, "He spared not their soul from death." What "the breath of life" is in Gen. 2:7, is explained for us in Gen. 7:22, where we read that every thing died, "all in whose nostrils was the breath of life." Margin, "Heb. the breath of the spirit of life," which is a still stronger expression, and is used of the whole animate creation that died in the Flood.

But such are the exigencies of Traditionalists, that in thirteen passages where the Hebrew word "*nephesh*" (soul) refers to a dead soul, such reference is hidden from the English reader by the Translators. *Nephesh* is actually rendered "body" in Lev. 21:11. Num. 6:6; 19:11, 13. Haggai 2:13. "Dead Body" in Num. 9:6, 7, 10. And "The Dead" in Lev. 19:28; 21:1; 22:4. Num. 5:2; 6:11. In none of these passages is there a word in the margin of either the A.V. or R.V. to indicate that the translators are thus rendering the Hebrew word *nephesh* (soul).

Again, *Sheol* is the Hebrew word used in the Old Testament for the grave, or death-state, and Hades is the corresponding Greek word for it in the New Testament. It is *Hades* in Luke 16:23; and not *Gehenna*, which means hell.

The Scriptures are also positive and numerous which declare the "Hades," where the Rich Man is said to be "buried" is always represented as a place of silence. "There is no work, nor device, nor knowledge in the grave (Heb. Sheol) whither thou goest" (Ecc. 9:10). But the rich man, here, was making devices, based on his knowledge. Of those who are there it is written, "Their love, and their hatred, and their envy is now perished; neither have they any more a portion for ever in anything that is done under the sun" (Ecc. 9:6). But the rich man is represented as having "love" for his brethren; and as having a "portion" in what is being done on earth.

Psalm 6:5 declares that

> *"In death there is no remembrance of Thee, In the grave (Heb. Sheol) who shall give Thee thanks?"*

Psalm 31:17, "Let them be silent in the grave" (Heb. *Sheol*). Psalm 115:17,

"The dead praise not the Lord; Neither any that go down into silence"

The Scriptures everywhere speak of the dead as destitute of knowledge or speech;

"What profit is there in my blood, when I go down to the pit? Shall the dust praise Thee? shall it declare Thy truth?" Psalm 30:9,

"Shall Thy lovingkindness be declared in the grave? or Thy faithfulness in destruction?" Psalm 88:11,

"For the grave cannot praise Thee, death can not celebrate Thee: They that go down into the pit cannot hope for Thy truth." Isaiah 38:18,

"The living, the living, he shall praise Thee, as I do this day: The father to the children shall make known Thy truth." Isaiah 38:19,

and as knowing nothing till resurrection. If these Scriptures are to be believed (as they most surely are), then it is clear that the teaching of Tradition is not true, which says that death is not death, but only life in some other form.

Hades means the 'grave' (Heb. *Sheol*): not in Heathen mythology, but in the Word of God. It was in *Hades* the Lord Jesus was put: for "He was buried." As to His Spirit, He said, "Father, into thy hands I commend my Spirit" (Luke 23:46). And as to His body, it was "laid in a sepulchre." Of this burial He says (Psalm 16:9): "Thou wilt not leave my soul (*i.e.* me. Myself) in *Sheol* (or *Hades*), Neither wilt Thou suffer Thy holy one to see corruption."

These two lines are strictly parallel; and the second expands and explains the first. Hence, *Sheol* (Greek, *Hades*) is the place where "corruption" is seen. And resurrection is the only way of exit from it. This is made perfectly clear by the Divine commentary on the passage in the New Testament. We read in Acts 2:31: "He (David) seeing this before spake of the resurrection of Christ, that his soul (*i.e.* he) was not left in Hades; neither his flesh did see corruption." To make it still more clear, it is immediately added, and expressly stated, that "David is not yet ascended into the heavens" (v. 34), and therefore had not been raised from the dead. Note, it does not say David's body, but David. This is another proof that resurrection is the only way of entrance into heaven.

But this passage (Psalm 16:10) is again referred to in Acts 13:34-37, and here we have the same important lesson restated: "And as concerning that he raised him up from the dead, now no more to return to corruption, he saith...thou shalt not suffer thine Holy One to see corruption...For David fell on sleep, and was laid unto his fathers, and saw corruption. But he whom God raised again saw no corruption." He saw it not, because He was raised from the dead, and thus brought out of the Sepulchre, where He had been "buried." This is the teaching of the Word of God. It knows nothing whatever of a "descent into hell" as separate, and distinct, from His burial. That is tradition pure and simple. Not one of the Ancient Creeds of the Church knew anything of it. Up to the seventh century they all said "And was buried" and nothing more. But the Creed used in the Church of Aquileia (A.D. 400), instead of saying "buried" had the words "he descended into hell," but only as an equivalent for "he was buried." This was of course quite correct.

These are the words of Bishop Pearson (Exposition of the Creed. Fourth Ed. 1857, pp. 402-3) "I observe that in the Aquileian Creed, where this article was first expressed, there was no mention of Christ's burial; but the words of their Confession ran thus, crucified under Pontius Pilate, he descended in inferna. From whence there is no question but the observation of Ruffinus (fl. 397), who first expounded it, was most true, that though the Roman and Oriental Creeds had not these words, yet they had the sense of them in the word buried. It appears, therefore, that the first intention of putting these words in the Creed was only to express the burial of our Saviour, or the descent of his body into the grave. In a note he adds that "the same may be observed in the Athanasian Creed, which has the descent, but not the Sepulchre (*i.e.* the burial)...Nor is this observable only in these two, but also in the Creed made at Sirmium, and produced at Ariminim" (A.D. 359).

By the incorporation of the words "he descended into hell" in the "Apostles' Creed" and the retention of the word "buried," Tradition obtained an additional "article of faith" quite distinct from the fact of the Lord's burial. This is not a matter of opinion, but a matter of history. Not only are these historical facts vouched for by Bishop Pearson, but by Archbishop Ussher, and in more recent times by the late Bishop Harold-Browne in his standard work on the Thirty-Nine Articles.

Those who have been brought up on "The Apostles' Creed" naturally read this spurious additional article "he descended into hell," into Luke 23:43 and I Peter 3:19, and of course find it difficult to believe that those passages have nothing whatever to do with that "descent." They are thus led into the serious error of substituting man's tradition for God's revelation. This tradition about "the descent into hell" led directly to a misunderstanding of I Peter 3:17-22. But note:

1. There is not a word about "hell," or *Hades*, in the passage.
2. The word "spirit," by itself, is never used, without qualification, of man in any state or condition; but it is constantly used of angels, of whom it is said, "He maketh his angels spirits," *i.e.* they are spiritual beings, while a man is a human being.
3. In spite of these being "in-prison spirits," they are taken to refer to men; notwithstanding that in the next Epistle (II Pet. 2:4) we read of "the angels that sinned," and of their being "cast down to Tartarus (not *Hades* or *Gehenna*), and delivered into chains of darkness to be reserved unto the judgment of the great day." It is surprising that, in the face of these two passages (II Pet. 2:4 and Jude 6, 7), which speak of angels (or spirits) being "in chains," anyone should ever have interpreted the "in-prison spirits" of I Pet. 3:19 as referring to human beings!
4. Moreover, the word "preached" does not, by itself, refer to the preaching of the Gospel. It is not "evangelize," which would be ευαγγελιζω (*evangelizo*). But is is χηρυσσω (*kerusso*), to proclaim as a herald, to make proclamation, and the context shows that this paragraph about Christ is intended as an encouragement. It begins with verse 17: "For it is better, if the will of God be so, that ye suffer for well-doing than for evil-doing. For Christ also suffered for sins, the just for the unjust, that he might bring us to God." Then it goes on to explain that as Christ suffered for well-doing, and not for evil-doing, they were to do the same; and if they did they would have, like Him, a glorious triumph. For though He was put to death in the flesh, yet He was made alive again in spirit (*i.e.* in a spiritual body, I Cor. 15:44): and in this He made such proclamation of His triumph that it reached even to Tartarus, and was heard there by the angels reserved in chains unto judgment. Never mind, therefore, if you are called to suffer. You will have a like glorious triumph."

No other explanation of this passage takes in the argument of the context; or complies with the strict requirements of the original text. Thus the support for the tradition about Christ's "descent into hell" as distinct from His being buried, vanishes from the Scriptures. Eph. 4:9 also speaks of the Lord's descent "into the lower parts of the earth" before His ascension "on high." But this word "of" here is what is called the genitive of apposition, by which "of the earth" explains what is meant by "the lower parts" and should be rendered "the lower parts," that is to say "the earth." For example: "the temple of his body" means "the temple," that is to say "his body" (John 2:21). "A sign of circumcision" means "a sign," that is to say "circumcision" (Romans 4:11). "The first fruits of the Spirit" means "the first fruits," that is to say "the Spirit" (Romans 8:23). "The earnest of the Spirit" means "the earnest," that is to say "the Spirit" (2 Cor. 5:5). "The bond of peace" means "the bond," which is "peace" (Eph. 4:3). "The breastplate of righteousness" means "the breastplate," which is "righteousness" (Eph. 4:14). So here it should be rendered "He descended into the lower parts (that is to say) the earth." If it means more than this it is not true, for He was "laid in a Sepluchre" and not in a grave in, or below, the Earth: His spirit being commended into the Father's hands. This descension stands in contrast with His ascension —"He that descended is the same also that ascended" (v. 10). It refers to His descent from heaven in Incarnation, and not to any descent as distinct from that, or from His burial.

But Tradition is only handing down of the Old Serpent's lie which deceived our first parents. God said, "Thou shalt SURELY die" (Gen. 2:17). Satan said "Thou shalt NOT surely die" (Gen. 3:4). And all Traditionalists and Spiritists agree with Satan in saying, "There is no such thing as death; it is only life in some other form."

God speaks of death as an "enemy" (I Cor. 15:26)
Man speaks of it as a friend.

God speaks of it as a terminus.
Man speaks of it as a gate.

God speaks of it as a calamity.
Man speaks of it as a blessing.

God speaks of it as a fear and a terror.
Man speaks of it as a hope.

God speaks of delivering from it as shewing "mercy."
Man, strange to say, says the same! and loses no opportunity of seeking such deliverance by using every means in his power.

In Phil. 2:27 we read that Epaphroditus "was sick unto death; but God had mercy on him." So that it was mercy to preserve Epaphroditus from death. This could hardly be called "mercy" if death were the "gate of glory," according to popular tradition.

In II Cor. 1:10, 11, it was deliverance of no ordinary kind when Paul himself also was "delivered from so great a death" which called for corresponding greatness of thanksgiving for God's answer to their prayers on his behalf. Moreover, he trusted that God would still deliver him. It is clear from II Cor. 5:4 that Paul did not wish for death: for he distinctly says "not for that we would be unclothed, but clothed upon (i.e. in resurrection and "change") that mortality might be swallowed up of life"; not of death. This is what he was so "earnestly desiring" (v. 2). True, in Phil. 1:21 some think Paul spoke of death as "gain," but we may ask, "Whose gain?" The answer is clear, for the whole context from verses 12-24 shows that Christ and His cause are the subjects to which he is referring; not himself. Paul's imprisonment had turned out to be for "the furtherance of the Gospel" (v. 12). His death might further it still more, and thus prove a "gain" for it. Verse 21 begins with "for" and is given in explanation of verse 20.

Hezekiah also had reason to praise God for delivering him from "the king of terrors." It was "mercy" shown to Epaphroditus; it was "a gift" to Paul; it was "love" to Hezekiah. He says (Isa. 38:17-19):

"Thou hast in love to my soul (*i.e.* to me) delivered it (*i.e.* me) from the pit (Heb. Bor, a rock-hewn sepulchre) of corruption. For thou has cast all my sins behind thy back. For the grave (Heb. Sheol) cannot praise thee, death cannot celebrate thee: They that go down into the pit cannot hope for thy truth. The living, the living, he shall praise thee, as I do this day."

On the other hand the death of Moses was permitted, for it was his punishment, therefore, there was no deliverance for him though he sought it (Deut. 1:37; 3:23, 27; 4:21, 22; 31:2). Surely it could have been no punishment if death is not death; but, as is universally held, the gate of paradise! In Phil. 1:21, death would have been Paul's "gain," for Paul was not on Pisgah, but in prison; and it would have been a happy issue out of his then afflictions.

So effectually has Satan's lie succeeded, and accomplished its purpose that, though the Lord Jesus said "I will come again and receive you unto myself," Christendom says, with one voice, "No! Lord. Thou needest not to come for me: I will die and come to Thee." Thus the blessed hope of resurrection and the coming of the Lord have been well nigh blotted out from the belief of the Churches; and the promise of the Lord been made of none effect by the ravages of Tradition. Men may write their books, and a Spiritist may entitle on "There is no death," etc. They may sing words and expressions which are foreign to the Scriptures, about "the Church triumphant." They may speak of having "passed on"; and about the "home-going"; and "the great beyond"; and the "border-land"; and "beyond the veil"; but against all this we set a special revelation from God, introduced by the prophetic formula, "the Word of the Lord."

> *"This we say unto you BY THE WORD OF THE LORD that we which are alive and remain shall not precede (R.V.) them which are asleep" (I Thess. 4:15).*

To agree with Tradition this ought to have been written, "shall not precede them which are already with the Lord." But this would have made nonsense; and there is nothing of that in the Word of God. There are many things in Scripture difficult; and hard to be understood; there are many Figures of Speech also; but there are no self-contradictory statements such as that would have been.

Moreover, we ought to note that this special Divine revelation was given for the express purpose that we might not be ignorant on this subject, as the heathen and Traditionalists were. This revelation of God's truth as to the state of the dead is introduced by the noteworthy words in verse 13: "I would not have you ignorant, brethren, concerning them that are asleep." Unless, therefore, we know what the Lord has revealed, we must all alike remain "ignorant." What is revealed here "by the Word of the Lord", is

(a) That as the Lord Jesus was brought again from the dead (Heb. 13:20), so will His people be. "If we believe that Jesus died, and rose again, even so (we believe that) them also which sleep in (R.V. marg. through) Jesus will God bring with him" (*i.e.* bring again from the dead), even as the Lord Jesus died and rose again" (v. 14).

(b) That we which are alive and remain till His coming shall not precede those who have fallen on sleep.

(c) And therefore they cannot be with the Lord before us (v. 15).

(d) The first thing to happen will be their resurrection. They are called "the dead in Christ." Not the living, but "the dead," for resurrection concerns only "the dead" (v. 16).

(e) The next thing is we, the living, shall be "caught up together with them to meet the Lord in the air" (v. 17). Not (as many people put it) to meet our friends, who are supposed to be already there; but to meet "the Lord Himself" (v. 17).

(f) Finally, it is revealed that this is the manner in which we shall be "with the Lord". The word is *houtos* thus, so, in this manner, and in no other way.

Those who do not know the truths here given by special Divine revelation have invented other ways of getting there. They say the "death is the gate of glory." God says that resurrection and ascension is the gate. It is the tradition that those who have fallen asleep are already in heaven that has given rise to the idea of "the Church Triumphant." But no such expression can be found in Scripture. Eph. 3:15 is supposed to teach or support it, when it speaks of "The whole family in heaven and earth." But it is by no means necessary to translate the words in this way. The R. V. and the American R.V. render them "every family in heaven and earth" so does the A.V. also in Eph. 1:21, where we have the same subject, viz. the giving of names (as ονομαζω *onomazo*, in both places, means. See Luke 6:13, etc.) to some of these heavenly families, *e.g.* "principality and power, and might, and dominion, and every name that is named, not only in this world, but in that which is to come." It is not "the whole family" that is named; but every family has its own name given to it. A few verses before Eph. 3:15 we have two more of these families, "principalities and powers" (v. 10). Why then create a new thing altogether by forcing verse 15 apart from its context? These families in heaven are clearly set in contrast with the family of God upon earth. In verse 10 the earthly family is used as an object lesson to the heavenly family.

Now, these being the positive and clear statements of revelation as to man in life and in death, there are certain passages in the New Testament which seem to speak with a different voice, and to bear a different testimony. We say advisedly "seem"; for when properly understood, and accurately translated, not only is there no difference or opposition to the teaching of the Old Testament, but there is perfect harmony and unity in their testimony. The one corroborates and supports the other. If not, meaning must be given to those passages which we have quoted above from the Old Testament: and Traditionalists must show us how they understand them; and support their interpretations by proofs from the Word of God.

There are five passages which are generally relied on and referred to by Traditionalists, *viz*:

(1) Matthew 22:32
"I am the God of Abraham, and the God of Isaac, and the God of Jacob? God is not the God of the dead, but of the living."

(2) Luke 23:43

"And Jesus said unto him, Verily I say unto thee, to day shalt thou be with me in paradise."

(3) II Corinthians 5:6,8

"Therefore we are always confident, know that, whilst we are at home in the body, we are absent from the Lord: We are confident, I say, and willing rather to be absent from the body, and to be present with the Lord."

(4) Philippians 1:23

"For I am in a strait betwixt two, having a desire to depart, and to be with Christ; which is far better:"

(5) Luke 16:19-31

"There was a certain rich man, which was clothed in purple and fine linen, and fared sumptuously every day: And there was a certain beggar named Lazarus, which was laid at his gate, full of sores, and desiring to be fed with the crumbs which fell from the rich man's table: moreover the dogs came and licked his sores. And it came to pass, that the beggar died, and was carried by the angels into Abraham's bosom: the rich man also died, and was buried; And in hell he lift up his eyes, being in torments, and seeth Abraham afar off, and Lazarus in his bosom. And he cried and said, Father Abraham, have mercy on me, and send Lazarus, that he may dip the tip of his finger in water, and cool my tongue; for I am tormented in this flame. But Abraham said, Son, remember that thou in thy lifetime receivedst thy good things, and likewise Lazarus evil things: but now he is comforted, and thou are tormented. And beside all this, between us and you there is a great gulf fixed: so that they which would pass from hence to you cannot; neither can they pass to us, that would come from thence. Then he said, I pray thee therefore, father, that thou wouldest send him to my father's house: For I have five brethren; that he may testify unto them, lest they also come into this place of torment. Abraham saith unto him, They have Moses and the prophets; let them hear them. And he said, Nay, father Abraham: but if one went unto them from the dead, they will repent. And he said unto him, if they hear not Moses and the prophets, neither will they be persuaded, though one rose from the dead."

(1) We will deal with them in this order. The first is "The God of the Living" (Matt. 22:32. Mark 12:27. Luke 20:38). In these scriptures it is stated that "God is not the God of the dead, but of the living." But Traditionalists, believing that the "dead" are "the living," making God the "God of the dead," which He distinctly says He is not. Interpreting the words in this way, they utterly ig-

nore the whole context, which shows that the words refer to the RESURRECTION, and not to the dead at all. Notice how this is emphasized in each Gospel:

(i) "Then come unto Him the Sadducees, which say there is no RESURRECTION" (Matt. 22:23. Mark 12:18. Luke 20:27).

(ii) The one issue raised by the Sadducees was the question, "Whose wife shall she be in the RESURRECTION?" (Matt. 22:28. Mark 12:23. Luke 20:33).

(iii) The answer of our Lord deals solely with this one issue, which was RESURRECTION. Hence He says: Matt. 22, "as touching the RESURRECTION of the dead" (v. 31). Mark 12, "as touching the dead that they RISE" (v. 26). Luke 20, "now that the dead are RAISED, even Moses showed at the bush, when he called the Lord, the God of Abraham, and the God of Isaac, and the God of Jacob, for he is not a God of the dead, but of the living, for all live unto him" (v. 38).

These words were spoken by the Lord Jesus in order to prove "that the dead are RAISED." Traditionalists use them to prove that the dead are "living" without being RAISED! The Sadducees may have denied many other things, but the one and the only thing in question here is RESURRECTION. Christ's argument was:

1. God's words at the bush prove a life for the dead patriarchs.

2. But there is no life for the dead without a resurrection.

3. Therefore they must be RAISED FROM THE DEAD; or "live again" by Him.

This argument held good, for it silenced the Sadducees. For if they are "living" now, and not dead, how does that prove a resurrection? And, moreover, what is the difference between them and those who are in "the land of the living"? For this is the expression constantly used of the present condition of life in contrast with the state of death.

Psalms 27:13

"I had fainted, unless I had believed to see the goodness of the Lord in the land of the living." Psalms 56:13 "For thou hast delivered my soul from death: wilt not thou deliver my feet from falling, that I may walk before God in the light of the living?" Psalms 116:9 "I will walk before the Lord in the land of the living."

Psalms 142:5

"I cried unto thee, O Lord: I said, Thou art my refuge and my portion in the land of the living."

Jeremiah 11:19

"But I was like a lamb or an ox that is brought to the slaughter; and I knew not that they had devised devices against me, saying, Let us destroy the tree with the fruit thereof, and let us cut him off from the land of the living, that his name may be no more remembered."

Ezekiel 26:20

"When I shall bring thee down with them that descend into the pit, with the people of old time, and shall set thee in the low parts of the earth, in places desolate of old, with them that go down to the pit, that thou be not inhabited; and I shall set glory in the land of the living;"

In this last passage the contrast is very pointed; where God speaks of bringing down to death and the grave and setting His glory "in the land of the living."

The argument as to resurrection was so conclusive to the Scribes who heard Him, that they said, "Master, thou has well said. And after that they durst not ask him any question at all" (Luke 20:39, 40).

(2) Luke 23:43: "To-day shalt thou be with me in Paradise." This can mean only "Verily I say unto thee this day, thou shalt be with me in Paradise."

In the first place we must remember that the punctuation is not inspired. It is only of human authority. There is none whatever in the Greek manuscripts. We have, therefore, perfect liberty to criticize and alter man's use of it, and to substitute our own. The verb "say" when used with "to-day," is sometimes separated from it by the word οτι *hoti* (that); and sometimes it is joined with it by the absence of *hoti*. The Holy Spirit uses these words with perfect exactness, and it behooves us to learn what He would thus teach us.

When He puts the word *hoti* (that) between "say" and "to-day," it throws "to-day" into what is said, and cuts it off from the verb "say," *e.g.* Luke 19:9, "Jesus said...that (Gr. *hoti*) this day is salvation come to this house." Here "to-day" is joined with the verb "come," and separated from the verb "I say." So also in Luke 4:21 "And he began to say unto them that (*hoti*) this day is this scripture fulfilled in your ears." Here again the presence of *hoti* cuts off "to-day" from "say" and joins it with "fulfilled."

But this is not the case in Luke 23:43. Here the Holy Spirit has carefully excluded the word *hoti* (that). How then dare anyone to read the verse as though He had not excluded it, and read it as though it said "I say unto thee, that this day," *etc.* It is surely adding to the Word of God to insert, or imply the insertion of the word "that" when the Holy Spirit has not used it; as He has in two other places in this same Gospel (Luke 4:21; 19:9).

We are now prepared to see that we must translate Luke 23:43 in this manner, "Verily I say to thee this day, thou shalt be with me in Paradise." The prayer was answered. It referred to the future, and so did the promise; for, when the Lord shall have come in His Kingdom, the only Paradise the Scripture knows of will be restored. As a matter of fact, the Greek word Paradise occurs in the Septuagint twenty-eight times. Nine times it represents the Hebrew word "Eden," and nineteen times the Hebrew word *Gan* (Garden). In English it is rendered "Eden," "Garden," "Forest," "Orchard." The Hebrew word for "Eden" occurs sixteen times. The Hebrew word for "Garden" is used of Eden thirteen times in Genesis alone; and six times in other passages, of "the garden of God," *etc*. See Gen. 2. Neh. 2:8. Ecc. 2:5. Song 4:13.

From these facts we learn and notice others:

(i) We see that the three words, Paradise, Eden, and Garden are used interchangeably; and always, either of the Eden of Gen. 2. or of some glorious park like beauty which may be compared with it.

(ii) It is never used in any other sense than that of an earthly place of beauty and delight.

(iii) The "tree of life" and the river of "the water of life" are its great conspicuous characteristics.

(iv) We see it Described in Gen. 2. Lost in Gen. 3. Restoration promised in Rev. 2:7. Regained in Rev. 22:1-5, 14, 17. Further we must note that the formula "I say unto thee this day," was a well known Hebrew idiom used to emphasized the solemnity of the occasion and the importance of the words. See Deut. 4:26, 29, 40; 5:6; 6:6; 7:11; 8:1, 11, 19; 9:3; 10:13; 11:2, 8, 13, 18, 27, 28, 32; 13:18; 15:5; 19:9; 26:3, 17, 18; 27:1, 4, 10; 28:1, 13, 14, 15; 24:12; 30:2, 8, 11, 15, 16, 18, 18; 32:46. The expression, therefore, "I say unto thee this day," marks the wonderful character of the man's faith; which, under such circumstances, could still believe in, and look forward to the coming kingdom; and acknowledge that Christ was the King, though on that very day He was hanging on the Cross.

(3) The third passage, II Cor. 5:6, 8, "to be absent from the body and to be present with the Lord," was the inspired desire of the Apostle, which could be realized only in resurrection. Resurrection (and not death) is the subject of the whole context. These words are generally misquoted "Absent from the body, present with the Lord," as though it said that when we are absent from the body we are present with the Lord. But no such sentence

can be found. No less than nine words are deliberately omitted from the context when the quotation is thus popularly made. The omission of these words creates quite a new sense, and puts the verse out of all harmony with the context; the object of which is to show that we cannot be "present with the Lord" except by being clothed upon with our RESURRECTION body, our "house which is from heaven."

We might with equal justice quote the words "hang all the law and the prophets," and leave out "on these two commandments" (Matt. 22:40); or say "there is no God" and leave out "The fool hath said in his heart" (Psalm 53:1), or say "Ye shall not drink wine," and leave out "Ye have planted pleasant vineyards, but (ye shall not drink wine) of them" (Amos 5:11); or talk about "the restitution of all things" and leave out "which God hath spoken by the mouth of all his holy prophets" (Acts 3:21).

All these partial quotations are correct so far as the Text is concerned, but what about the Context? The context is, "We are confident, I say, and willing rather to be absent from the body, and to be present with the Lord" (v. 8).

By omitting the words printed in italics the sense is entirely changed. Being "at home in the body" in both verses is explained, in verse 4 as being in "this tabernacle," which, in v. 1, is called "our earthly house of this tabernacle"; and being "present (or at home with) the Lord" is explained in verse 2 as being "clothed upon with our house which is from heaven." The Apostle distinctly says, on the one hand, that he did not wish to die (v. 4, "not that we would be unclothed"); and on the other hand, he was not merely "willing rather" but "earnestly desiring to be clothed upon" (v.2). It is true that some years later he did say "to die is gain"; but as we have seen above, the circumstances were very different, for he was then in prison.

(4) This brings us to the expression of Paul's desire in Phil. 1:23. The desire of the Apostle was not "to depart" himself, by dying; but his desire was for the return of Christ; the verb rendered "depart" being used elsewhere in the New Testament only in Luke 12:36, where it is rendered "return": "when he shall RETURN from the wedding." May we not fairly ask, "Why are we not to translate it in the same way in Phil. 1:23?"

The preposition ανα *ana* (again), when compounded with the verb λυω *luo* (to loosen), means to loosen back again to the place from whence the original departure was made, not to set out to a new place; hence, αναλυω *analuo* means to loosen back again or to return, and it is so rendered in the only other place where it occurs in the New Testament, Luke 12:36: "when he shall RETURN from the wedding." It does

NOT mean to depart, in the sense of setting off from the place where one is, but to return to the place that one has left. The noun αναλυςις analusis occurs in II Tim. 4:6, and has the same meaning, returning or dissolution, *i.e.* the body returning to dust as it was, and the spirit returning to God who gave it. The verb does not occur in the Greek translation of the Canonical books of the Old Testament, but it does occur in the Apocryphal books which, though of no authority in the establishment of doctrine, are invaluable, as to the use and meaning of words. In these books this word always means to return, and is generally so translated.

But there is another fact with regard to Phil. 1:23. The English verb depart occurs 130 times in the New Testament; and is used as the rendering of 22 different Greek words. But this one verb analuo occurs only twice, and is rendered depart only once; the other occurrence being rendered return, and used by the Lord Himself of His own return from heaven. We must also further note that it is not the simple infinitive of the verb *to return*. It is a combination of three words: the preposition ειϛ *eis* (unto), and the definite article το *to* (the), with the aorist inference αναλυσαι *analusai* (to return); so that the verb must be translated as a noun—"having a strong desire unto THE RETURN"; *i.e.* of Christ, as in Luke 12:36. These words must be interpreted by the context, and from this it is clear that the Apostle's whole argument is that the Gospel might be furthered (v. 12); and that Christ might be magnified (v. 20). To this end he cared not whether he lived or died; for, he says, "to me, living (is) Christ, and dying (would be) gain. But if living in the flesh (would be Christ), this (dying) for me, (would be) the fruit of (my) labour. Yet, what I shall choose I wot not, for I am being PRESSED OUT OF these two [*i.e.* living or dying (vv. 20, 21), by a third thing (v. 23), viz.], having a strong desire unto THE RETURN (*i.e.* of Christ), and to be with Christ, which is a far, far better thing". (The word εκ *ek* occurs 857 times, and is never once translated "betwixt" except in this place. It is translated "out of" 165 times).

Paul's imprisonment had made many brethren "more abundantly bold" (v. 12 R.V.) to preach the gospel. His death might produce still more abundant fruit of his labor; for these brethren were the fruit of his labor (v. 11; 4:17. Romans 1:13). Christ would thus be magnified in his body whether Paul lived or died. That was why he did not know what to choose of these three things: Living would be good; for he could himself preach Christ. Dying might be even better, and further the preaching of Christ more abundantly, judging by the result of his imprisonment. But there was a third thing, which was far, far better than either; and that was the return of Christ, which he so earnestly desired.

It is for the Traditionalists to show how they deal with these facts. It is not sufficient to say they do not believe in this our understanding of these passage: they must show how they dispose of our evidence, and must produce their own support of their own conclusions. Here we have four passages which seem to be opposed to those we have quoted from the Old Testament. Both cannot be true. We must either explain away the Old Testament passages, or we must see whether these four passages admit of other renderings, which remove their apparent opposition. We have suggested these other renderings, based on ample evidence; which, not only deprive them of such opposition, but show that their teaching is in exact accordance with those other passages.

(5) There remains a fifth passage, Luke 16:19-31, commonly called "the Parable of the Rich Man and Lazarus," or of "Dives and Lazarus." (If we speak of it sometimes as a Parable, it is not because we hold it to be one of Christ's Parables, specially so called, but because it partakes of the nature of parabolic teaching.)

It is absolutely impossible that the Traditional interpretation of this can be correct, because if it were, it would be directly opposed to all other teaching of Scripture. And the Lord's words cannot and must not be so interpreted. If it be Bible truth (as it is) that "the dead know not anything," how could the Lord have taught, and how can we believe that they do know a very great deal? If it be that fact that when man's "breath goeth forth, in that very day his thoughts perish," how can we believe that he goes on thinking? and not only thinking without a brain, but putting his "thoughts" into words, and speaking them without a tongue?

When the great subject of Resurrection is in question, one of the most solemn arguments employed is that, if there be no such thing as resurrection, then not only all the dead, but "they also which are fallen asleep in Christ are perished" (I Cor. 15:18). This is also the argument which immediately follows in verse 29 (after the parenthesis in verses 20-28), and is based upon verse 18. "Else, what are they doing who are being baptized? It is for dead (corpses) if the dead rise not at all. Why are they then being baptized for corpses?" Which is, of course, the case, if they are not going to rise again. We render this as Romans 8:10, 11 is rendered, by supplying the ellipsis of the verb "to be", as in both the A.V. and the R.V. The word νεκροι *nekroi* with the article (as in I Cor. 15:29) means dead bodies, or corpses. See Gen. 23:3, 4, 6, 8, 13, 15. Deut. 28:26. Jer. 12:3. Ezek. 37:9. Matt. 22:31. Luke 24:5. I Cor. 15:29 (1st and 3rd words), 35, 42, 52.

On the other hand, *nekroi* without the article (as in I Pet. 4:6) means dead people, *i.e.* people who have died. See Deut. 14:1. Matt. 22:32. Mark 9:10. Luke 16:30, 31; 24:46. Acts 23:6; 24:15; 26:8. Romans 6:13; 10:7; 11:15. Heb. 11:19; 13:20. I Cor. 15:12, 13, 15, 16, 20, 21, 29 (2nd word), 32. This throws light upon I Pet. 4:6 (where it is without the article), which shows that "the dead," there, are those who had the gospel preached to them while they were alive, and though, according to the will of God, man might put them to death, they would "live again" in resurrection. The word μεν (*men*), though, is left untranslated, both in A.V. and R.V., as it is in I Pet. 3:18.

The word ζαω (*zao*), to live again, has for one of its principle meanings, to live in resurrection life. See Matt. 9:18. Acts 9:41. Mark 16:11. Luke 24:5, 23. John 11:25, 26. Acts 1:3; 25:19. Romans 6:10; 14:9. II Cor. 13:4. Rev. 1:18; 2:8; 13:14; 20:4, 5.

We are expressly enjoined by the Lord Himself: "Marvel not at this: for the hour is coming in the which all that are in the graves shall hear His voice" (John 5:28). These are the Lord's own words, and they tell us where His Voice will be heard; and, that is not in heaven, not in Paradise, or in any so-called "intermediate state," but "in the GRAVES." With this agrees Dan. 12:2, which tells us that those who "awake" in resurrection will be those "that sleep in the dust of the earth." It does not say, in "Abraham's bosom," or any other place, state, or condition, but "IN THE DUST OF THE EARTH"; from which man was "taken" (Gen. 2:7; 3:23), and to which he must "return" (Gen. 3:19. Ecc. 12:7).

It is of course, most blessedly true that there is a vast difference between the saved and the unsaved in this "falling asleep." The former have received the gift of "eternal life" (Romans 6:23): not yet in actual fruition; but "in Christ," who is responsible to raise them from the dead (John 6:39), that they may enter upon the enjoyment of it. The unsaved do not possess "eternal life," for it is declared to be "the gift of God" (Romans 6:23). Very different, therefore, are these two cases. The Atonement and Resurrection, and Ascension of Christ has made all the difference for His people. They die like others; but for them it is only falling asleep. Why? Because they are to wake again. Though dead, they are now called "the dead in Christ," but it remains perfectly true that "we who are alive and remain to the coming of the Lord shall not precede (R.V.) them." And, therefore, it follows, of necessity, that they cannot precede us.

But it is sometimes urged that "the Lord led forth a multitude of captives from Hades to Paradise when He wrested from Satan his power over death and Hades" (Eph. 4:8). But the fact is that Eph. 4:8 says nothing about Hades or Paradise! Nothing about "multitudes of captives," and nothing about the state between the moment of His dying and rising. It was "when He ascended up on high" that there was this great triumph for the Lord Jesus Christ. We are not told what were all the immediate effects of Christ's death, resurrection and ascension, in Satan's realm of evil angels. Col. 2:15 tells us the great fact that He "spoiled principalities and powers." Henceforth He held the keys of death and the grave (*Hades*):

Revelation 1:18

"I am he that liveth, and was dead; and behold, I am alive for evermore, Amen; and have the keys of hell and of death."

There was a mighty conflict and a glorious victory when Christ rose from the dead and conquered him that had the power of death. In proof and token of His triumph "many" (not a few) rose from the dead (Matt. 27:52, 53); but as other that have been raised from the dead again sleep in Christ awaiting the return and the final Resurrection.

We now come to the so-called Parable itself. It is evident that this Scripture (Luke 16:19-31) must be interpreted and understood in a manner that shall not only not contradict that plain and direct teaching of all these passages; but on the contrary, in a manner which must be in perfect and complete harmony with them: and in such a way that it shall be necessary for the better understanding of the whole context in which it stands. That is to say, we must not explain the Parable apologetically, as though we wished it were not there; but as though we could not do without it. We must treat it as being indispensable, when taken with the context.

Let us look first at some of the inconsistencies of the Traditional Interpreters. Some of them call it a "Parable"; but the Lord does not so designate it. It does not even begin by saying "He said." It commences abruptly—"There was"; without any further guide as to the reason or meaning of what is said. Then they follow their own arbitrary will, picking out one word or expression, which they say is literal; and another, which they say is parabolic. For example, "Abraham's bosom" is, according to them, parabolic; and denotes Paradise. They are bound so to take it, because if literal, "Abraham's bosom" would hold only one person! It refers to the act of reclining at meals, where any one person, if he leaned back, would be "in the bosom" of the other. John was so placed with regard to the Lord Jesus (John 13:23; 21:20), and it was a token of favor and love (John 19:26; 20:2; 21:7). Then they take the "fire" and

the "water," the "tongue" and the "flame," etc., as being literal; but when
the Lord elsewhere speaks of "the worm that dieth not," they take that as
parabolic, and say it does not mean "a worm" but conscience. In all this
they draw only on their imagination, and interpret according to their
own arbitrary will.

If we follow out this illogical principle, then according to them Lazarus was never buried at all; while the rich man was. For "the rich man
also died and was buried" (v. 22); while Lazarus, instead of being buried,
was "carried by the angels into Abraham's bosom." There is the further
difficulty as to how a man who has been actually buried, could think
without a brain, or speak without a tongue. How can the spirit speak,
or act apart from the physical organs of the body? This is a difficulty our
friends cannot get over: and so they have to invent some theory (which
outdoes the Spiritists' invention of an "Astral body") which has no foundation whatever in fact: and is absolutely destitute of anything worthy of
the name "evidence" of any kind whatsoever. Then again, Hades is never
elsewhere mentioned as a place of fire. On the contrary, it is itself to be
"cast into the lake of fire" (Rev. 20:14).

Moreover, there is this further moral difficulty; in this parable, which
is supposed to treat of the most solemn realities as to the eternal destiny
of the righteous and the wicked, there is a man who receives all blessing,
and his only merit is poverty. That, for ought that is said, is the only title
Lazarus has for his reward. It is useless to assume that he might have been
righteous as well as poor. The answer is that the parable does not say a
word about it; and it is perfectly arbitrary for anyone to insert either the
words or the thought. On the other hand, the only sin for which the rich
man was punished with those torments was his previous enjoyment of
"good things" and his neglect of Lazarus. But for this neglect, and his style
of living, he might have been as good and moral a man as Lazarus.

Again, if "Abraham's bosom" is the same as Paradise, then we ask, "Is
that where Christ and the thief went according to the popular interpretation of Luke 23:43? Did they go to 'Abraham's bosom'"? The fact is,
the more closely we look at Tradition, the more glaring are the inconsistencies which it creates.

The teaching of the Pharisees had much in common with the teaching
of Romanists and Spiritists in the present day. We have only to refer to the
Lord's words to see what He thought of the Pharisees and their teachings.
He reserved for them His severest denunciations and woes; and administered to them His most scathing judgments. It was the teaching of the
Pharisees, which had made the Word of God of none effect, that was the

very essence of their sin and its condemnation. Everywhere the Lord refers to this as bringing down His wrath; and calling forth His "woes."

The Word of God said one thing, and the Pharisees said another; they thus contracted themselves out of the Law of God by their traditions. The context shows that the Lord's controversy with the Pharisees was now approaching a crisis. It begins, in chapter 14:35, with the solemn formula, "He that hath ears to hear, let him hear." We are immediately shown who had these opened ears; for we read (15:1), "THEN drew near unto him all the publicans and sinners for to hear him. And the Pharisees and Scribes murmured, saying, This man receiveth sinners and eateth with them." They professed to have the key of knowledge, but they entered not in themselves; and those who were entering in they hindered (Matt. 23:13-33). They had the Scriptures, but they overlaid them with their traditions, and thus made them of none effect (Matt. 15:19). They were like "the Unjust Steward" (Luke 16:1-12) in the parable which immediately follows Luke 15. For He would explain to His immediate believing followers the iniquity of these murmuring Pharisees. They dealt unjustly with the oracles of God which were committed unto them (Rom. 3:2). They allowed His commandments to be disobeyed by others that they might make gain. In Mark 7:9 the Lord said, "Full well ye reject (Margin, frustrate) the commandment of God, that ye may keep your own tradition." This was said in solemn irony; for they did not "well" in the strict meaning of the word, though they did well, i.e. consistently with their own teaching when they practically did away with the fifth and seventh Commandments for their own profit and gain, just as Rome in later days did away with the doctrine of "justification through faith" by the sale of "indulgences." (Read carefully Matt. 15:3-6 and Mark 7:7-13). They were "unjust stewards"; and contrary to their teaching, the Lord declared there was no such thing as "little" or "much" when it cam to honesty, especially in dealing with the Word of God; and that, if they were unfaithful in the least, they would be in much also, and could not be trusted. The time was at hand when the sentence would go forth, "thou mayest be no longer steward."

Then in Luke 16:14 we read: "The Pharisees also, who were covetous, heard all these things; and they derided him" (v. 14): lit., they turned up their noses at Him! Compare chapter 23:35, "The rulers scoffed at him." The same word as in Psalm 22:7, "All they that see me laugh me to scorn." The supreme moment had come. We may thus paraphrase His words which follow and lead up to the Parable: "You deride and scoff at Me, as if I were mistaken, and you were innocent. You seek to justify yourselves before men, but God knoweth your hearts. You highly esteem your traditions, but they are abomination in the sight of God (v. 15). The law and the prophets were until John, but you deal unjustly with them, changing them and wresting them at your pleasure, by your tradition, and by the false glosses ye have put upon them. And when John preached the Kingdom of God, every one used violence and hostility against it by contradictions, persecution, and derision (v. 16). And yet, though by your vain traditions you would make the law void and of none effect, it is easier for heaven and earth to pass away, than for one tittle of the law to fail (v. 17). Take one instance out of many. It is true that God permitted, and legislated for, divorce. But ye, by your traditions and arbitrary system of divorces, have degraded it for gain. Nevertheless, that law still remains, and will stand for ever, and he who accepts your teaching on the subject, and receives your divorces, and marrieth another, committeth adultery" (v. 18).

Then the Lord immediately passes on to the culminating point of His lesson (v. 19): "There was a certain rich man," etc. He makes no break. He does not call it, or give it as one of His own Parables; but He at once goes on to give another example from the traditions of the Pharisees, in order to judge them out of their own mouth. A parable of this kind need not be true in itself, or in fact; though it must be believed to be true by the hearers, if not by the speaker. No more than Jotham's parable of the Trees speaking (Judges 9:7-15). No more than when the Pharisees, on another occasion, said "this fellow doth not cast out devils but by Beelzebub, the prince of the devils"; and He, judging them out of their own mouth, did not contradict them, nor did He admit the truth of their words when He replied, "If I by Beelzebub cast out devils, by whom do your children cast them out?" (Matt. 12:24-27). No! the Lord did not bandy words in argument with these arch-Traditionists, but turned the tables upon them. It was the same here, in Luke 16. He neither denied nor admitted the truth of their tradition when He used their own teachings against themselves. These are the "offences" of chapter 17.

It was the same in the case of the parable of the "pounds" a little later on, when He said, "Out of thine own mouth will I judge thee, thou wicked servant. Thou knewest that I was an austere man, taking up what I laid not down, and reaping that I did not sow" (Luke 19:22). The Lord was not, of course, an austere and unjust man; but He uses the words which those to whom He was speaking believed to be true; and condemned them out of their own mouth.

We believe that the Lord is doing the very same thing here. The framework of the illustration is exactly what the Pharisees believed and taught.

It is a powerful and telling example of one of their distinctive traditions, by which they made the teaching of God's Word of none effect. It is, of course, adapted by the Lord so as to convey His condemnation of the Pharisees. He represents the dead as speaking, but the words put into Abraham's mouth contain the sting of what was His own teaching. In verse 18 He had given an example of their PRACTICE in making void the Law of God as to marriage and divorce; and in the very next verse (19) He proceeds to give an example of their Doctrine to show how their traditions made void the truth of God; using their very words as an argument against themselves; and showing, by His own words, which He puts into Abraham's mouth (verses 29 and 31), that all these traditions were contrary to God's truth.

They taught that the dead could go to and communicate with the living; the Lord declares that this is impossible; and that none can go "from the dead" but by resurrection; "neither will they be persuaded, though one rose from the dead" (v. 31). Note, these latter are His own words; He knew that their traditions were false, and in this very parable He corrects them. He distinctly declares that no dead person could go to the living except by resurrection; and that if one did go it would be useless; for, there was one of the same name – Lazarus, who was raised from the dead shortly afterward, but their reply was to call a Council, in which "they determined to put Lazarus also to death," as well as Himself (John 12:10). And when the Lord rose from the dead they again took counsel, and would not believe (Matt. 28:11-15). Thus the parable is made by the Lord to give positive teaching as well as negative, and to teach the truth as well as to correct error.

In the Talmud we have those very traditions gathered up which the Lord refers to in His condemnation. Many are there preserved which were current in our Lord's day. We can thus find out exactly what these popular traditions were. "Paradise," "The carrying away by angels," "Abraham's bosom," etc., were the popular expressions constantly used. Christ was not the first who used these phrases, but He used the language of the Pharisees, turning it against them. Take a few examples from the Talmud:

(1) In Kiddushin (Treatise on Betrothal), fol. 72, there is quoted from Juchasin, fol. 75, 2, a long story about what Levi said of Rabbi Judah: "This day he sits in Abraham's bosom," *i.e.* the day he died.

There is a difference here between the Jerusalem and the Babylonian Talmuds – the former says Rabbi Judah was "carried by angels"; the latter says that he was "placed in Abraham's bosom."

Here we have again the Pharisees' tradition as used against them by our Lord.

(2) There was a story of a woman who had seen six of her sons slain (we have it also in II Macc. 7). She heard the command given to kill the youngest (two- and-a-half years old), and running into the embraces of her little son, kissed him and said, "Go thou, my son, to Abraham my father, and tell him 'Thus saith thy mother. Do not thou boast, saying, I built an altar, and offered my son Isaac. For thy mother hath built seven altars, and offered seven sons in one day," etc. (Midrash Echah, fol. 68.1).

(3) Another example may be given out of a host of others (Midrash on Ruth, fol. 44, 2; and Midrash on Coheleth (Ecclesiastes) fol. 86, 4). "There are wicked men, that are coupled together in this world. But one of them repents before death, the other doth not, so one is found standing in the assembly of the just, the other in the assembly of the wicked. The one seeth the other and saith, 'Woe! And Alas! There is accepting of persons in this thing. He and I robbed together, committed murder together; and now he stands in the congregation of the just, and I, in the congregation of the wicked.' They answered him: 'O thou foolish among mortals that are in the world! Thou weft abominable and cast forth for three days after thy death, and they did not lay thee in the grave; the worm was under thee, and the worm covered thee; which, when this companion of thine came to understand, he became a penitent. It was in thy power also to have repented, but thou dist not'. He saith to them, 'Let me go now, and become a penitent'. But they say, 'O thou foolishest of men, dost thou not know, that this world in which thou are, is like a Sabbath, and the world out of which thou comest is like the evening of the Sabbath? If thou does not provide something on the evening of the Sabbath, what wilt thou eat on the Sabbath day? Dost thou not know that the world out of which thou camest is like the land; and the world, in which thou now art, is like the sea? If a man make no provision on land for what he should eat at sea, what will he have to eat?' He gnashed his teeth, and gnawed his own flesh." (

4) We have examples also of the dead discoursing with one another; and also with those who are still alive (Beracoth, fol. 18, 2– *Treatise on Blessings*). "R. Samuel Bar Nachman saith, R. Jonathan saith, How doth it appear that the dead have any discourse among themselves? It appears from what is said (Deut. 34:4), And the Lord said unto him, This is the land, concerning which I sware unto Abraham, to Isaac, and to Jacob, saying." What is the meaning of the word saying? The Holy Blessed God saith unto Moses, 'Go thou and say to Abraham, Isaac, and Jacob, the

oath which I sware unto you, I have performed unto your children'."
Note that 'Go thou and say to Abraham,' *etc.*

Then follows a story of a certain pious man that went and lodged in a
burying place, and heard two souls discoursing among themselves. "The
one said unto the other, 'Come, my companion, and let us wander about
the world, and listen behind the veil, what kind of plagues are coming
upon the world'. To which the other replied, 'O my companion, I cannot; for I am buried in a can mat; but do thou go and whatsoever thou
hearest, do thou come and tell me'," etc. The story goes on to tell of the
wandering of the soul and what he heard, *etc.*

(5) There was a good man and a wicked man that died; as for the good
man, "he had no funeral rites solemnized"; but the wicked man had.
Afterward, there was one who saw in his dream, the good man walking
in gardens, and hard by pleasant springs; but the wicked man "with his
tongue trickling drop by drop, at the bank of a river, endeavouring to
touch the water, but he could not." (Chagigah, fol. 77. Treatise on Exodus 23:17).

(6) As to "the great gulf", we read (Midrash [or Commentary] on
Coheleth [Ecclesiastes], 103. 2), "God hath set the one against the other
(Ecc. 7:14) that is Gehenna and Paradise. How far are they distant? A
hand-breadth". Jochanan saith, "A wall is between", but the Rabbis say
"They are so even with one another, that they may see out of one into
the other".

The traditions set forth above were widely spread in many early Christian writings, showing how soon the corruption spread which led on to
the Dark Ages and to all the worst errors of Romanism. The Apocryphal
books (written in Greek, not in Hebrew, Cents. i and ii B.C.) contained
the germ of this teaching. That is why the Apocrypha is valued by Traditionalists, and is incorporated by the Church of Rome as an integral part
of her Bible.

The *Apocrypha* contains prayers for the dead; also "the song of the
three Children" (known in the Prayer Book as the Benedicite), in which
"the spirits and souls of the righteous" are called on to bless the Lord.

The *Te Deum*, also, which does not date further back than the fifth
century, likewise speaks of the Apostles and Prophets and Martyrs as
praising God now.

From all this it seems to us perfectly clear that the Lord was not delivering this as a Parable, or as His own direct teaching; but that He was
taking the current, traditional teachings of the Pharisees, which He was
condemning; and using them against themselves, thus convicting them

out of their own mouths. We are quite aware of the objection which will occur to some of our readers. But it is an objection based wholly on human reasoning, and on what appears to them to be probable. It will be asked, is it possible that our Lord would give utterance in such words without giving some warning to us as to the way to which He used them? Well, the answer to such is that, warning has been given in the uniform and unanimous teaching of Scripture. His own words: "they have Moses and the Prophets, let them hear them," addressed to the Pharisees through "the Rich Man" may be taken as addressed to us also. We have (as they had) the evidence of the Old Testament (in "Moses and the Prophets"), and we have also the evidence of the New Testament, which accords with the Old. If we "hear them," it would be impossible for us to suppose, for a moment, that Christ could be teaching here, that which is the very opposite to that of the whole Word of God.

We have the Scriptures of truth; and they reveal to us, in plain, direct, categorical, unmistakable words, that "the dead know not anything"; and that when man's breath goeth forth, "in that very day his thoughts perish." It is taken for granted, therefore, that we shall believe what God says in these and many other passages of His Word; and had we not ab-sorbed tradition from our earliest years we should have at once seen that the popular interpretation of this passage is quite contrary to the whole analogy of Scripture. We ought to discern, at the very first glance at it, that it is unique, and stands out so isolated, by itself, that we should nev-er for one moment dream of accepting as truth that which, if we know anything of His Word, we should instantly and instinctively detect as human tradition used for a special purpose. But, unfortunately, we have been brought up for the most part on man's books, instead of the Bible. People draw their theology from hymns written by men who were satu-rated with tradition; who, when they did write a good hymn generally spoiled it in the last verse, by setting "death" as the church's hope, instead of Christ's coming. Hence, hymns are solemnly sung which contain such absurd, paradoxical teaching as the singing of God's praises while our tongues are seeing corruption, and "lie silent in the grave."

Persons saturated with such false traditions come to this Scripture with minds filled with the inventions, fabrications, and imaginations of man; and can, of course, see nothing but their own traditions apparently sanctioned by our Lord. They do not notice the fact that in the very par-able itself the Lord corrected the false doctrine by introducing the truth of resurrection. But when we read the passage in the light of the whole Word of God, and especially in the light of the context, we see in it the traditions of the Pharisees, which were "highly esteemed among men," but were *"abomination in the sight of God"* (v. 15).

All these traditions passed into Romanism. This is why we read in the note of the English Romish Version (the Douay) on Luke 16: "The bosom of Abraham is the resting place of all them that died in perfect state of grace before Christ's time – heaven, before, being shut from men. It is called in Zachary a lake without water, and sometime a prison, but most commonly, of the Divines, 'Limbus Patrum', for that it is thought to have been the higher part, or brim, of hell," etc. Our Protestant friends do not recognize this fact; and hence they have not wholly purged themselves from Romish error. The Jews corrupted their religion by taking over the Pagan teachings of Greek Mythology. Romanism adopted these Jewish traditions of prayers for the dead and added others of her own; and the Reformed Churches took over Romish traditions connected with the so-called "Intermediate State," which they should have purged out.

Instead of completing the Reformation in respect to such heathen traditions, they are still clinging to them to-day; and so tenaciously, that they are giving Romanists and Spiritists all they want as the foundation for their false teachings; while they reserve their wrath for those who, like ourselves, prefer to believe God's truth in opposition to the first great lie of the Old Serpent. But once see the truth of God's word, that "death" means death; and cease to read the word as meaning life – and away goes the only ground for the worship of the Virgin Mary, the invocation of saints, prayers to or for the dead; and all the vapourings and falsehoods of "lying spirits" and "teachings of demons" (I Tim. 4:1, 2), who would deceive, by personating deceased persons of whom God declares their thoughts have perished. But there is one further argument which we may draw from the internal evidence of the passage itself, taken with other statements in the Gospel narrative. The Jews laid great stress on the fact that they were "Abraham's seed" (John 8:33). They said, "Abraham is our Father," whereupon the Lord answers that, though they might be Abraham's seed according to the flesh, yet they were not Abraham's true seed, inasmuch as they did not the works of Abraham (vv. 39, 40).

Early in the Gospels this fallacy was dealt with judicially, when John said by the Holy Spirit: "Think not to say within yourselves, We have Abraham to our father" (Matt. 3:9). This was when He saw many of the Pharisees and Sadducees come to His baptism; and called them "a generation of vipers," and not the sons of Abraham. They thought and believed that inasmuch as they were the sons of Abraham by natural generation, they were entitled to all the blessings and privileges which were given to Abraham and his seed. So here, one of them is represented as saying, "Father Abraham." Three times he calls him "father," as though to lay claim to these blessings and privileges (vv. 24, 27, 30). And the point of the Lord's teaching is this, that the first time Abraham speaks, he is made to acknowledge the natural relationship—"Son," he says (v. 25). But he repudiates the Pharisee's title to any spiritual favor on that account. He does not use the word "Son" again. Abraham is represented as repudiating the Pharisee's claim to anything beyond natural relationship. He may be related to him according to the flesh, but there is no closer relationship, though the Pharisee continues to claim it. So the Lord does not make Abraham repeat the word "Son" again; though the rich man twice more calls Abraham "Father."

This understanding of the passage is, therefore, in strictest harmony with the whole of the immediate context, and with all other Scriptures which bear upon this subject. It was quite unnecessary for the Lord to stop to explain for us the sense in which He used this tradition, because it was so contrary to all the other direct statements of Scripture, that no one ought for a moment to be in doubt as to what is the scope of the Lord's teaching here. No previous knowledge of Pharisaic traditions is necessary for the gathering of this scope. But as this is the conflict between Tradition and Scripture, the evidence from the Talmud comes in, and may well be used to strengthen our interpretation.

No! the Lord was at the crisis of His condemnation of the Pharisees for their false traditions which made the Word of God of none effect, and He makes use of those very teachings, adapting them to the great end of condemning them out of their own mouth.

May we all prayerfully consider the testimony of God's Word in regard to death and when the dead will live again. Thanks be to God in that we have the victory through Jesus Christ our Lord and that victory is in Him for truly He is the Resurrection and The Life.

Crucified with Christ

"I am crucified with Christ, nevertheless I live, yet not I, but Christ liveth in me; and the life which I now live in the flesh I live by the faith of the Son of God, Who loved me and gave Himself for me." (Galatians 2:20).

"God forbid that I should glory, save in the cross of our Lord Jesus Christ, by whom the world is crucified unto me, and I unto the world. For in Christ Jesus neither circumcision availeth any thing nor uncircumcision, but a new creature" (Galatians 6:14,15).

These last words the Apostle Paul sums up his important letter to the churches of Galatia, and he emphasizes the great sum and substance, the essence and marrow of the Gospel of Christ, and of true Christianity. This is utterly and entirely opposed to the world and to the world's religion. The world is that which is opposed to the Father (I John 2:16). The world has always been willing to support religion, and even Christianity, provided it has been allowed to alter it, and adapt it, and put its own marks upon it. And in all ages Christians have been willing to comply with this condition, and have allowed its sacred deposits to be tampered with. To such St. Paul says, "As many as desire to make a fair show in the flesh, they constrain you to be circumcised; only lest they should suffer persecution for the cross of Christ" (Galatians 6:12). It was the fear of the world that constrained Christians to submit to circumcision. They allowed themselves to be made bad Jews lest they should be persecuted for being good Christians. "Marvel not," said Christ, "if the world hate you"; but His followers grew weary of being despised and hated, and so they listened to the world's overtures of peace, and accepted the world's terms to gain for themselves the world's security and luxury. But the world has ever broken its promise, and will yet break it more and more! "The friendship of the world is enmity with God." We cannot purchase peace with the world without losing peace with God. Its last work will be to strip and destroy that church, which has purchased peace at the cost of disobedience to the Lord and by compliance with the requirements of man! St. Paul's counsel here is, that mere religion without Christ is nothing, is useless, is worthless. Circumcision is useless without Christ, and uncircumcision is useless without Christ, *i.e.*, the old nature in any shape is nothing. Man's thought ever is that it is something, that something can be made of it. Hence no effort-has been spared. In one age restraint has been tried, in another, liberty. In one age discipline cuts it down, in another, indulgence lets it grow. One school advises , and tries monasticism, another believes in the development of man, but no modification of the natural man will suffice; it must be a "new creation" (II Corinthians 5:17, R. V., margin).

We must be made new

Man must be made over again, made anew. This is the great point on which the Apostle lays such stress here. He says, "From henceforth let no man trouble! me, for I bear in my body the
marks of the Lord Jesus" (Galatians 6:17). There is a double reference in his words, when translated more closely, "Administer not to me your cuts." I need them not, I am crucified with Christ. It is not marks nor brands made by man upon the flesh that we want, but it is the brands of the Lord Jesus. He was crucified for us, "wounded for our iniquities," and those who are crucified with Christ have His marks on them, and to such can be said, "the grace of our Lord Jesus Christ be with your spirit (verse 18). This is the cry from Heaven to all who are crucified with Christ, this "grace" in them and with them is the "mark" and "brand" which the world will never countenance and approve.

The world threatens with loss all who are thus marked as the Lord's. But what says He to such? "Seek first the Kingdom of God and His righteousness and all these things shall be added unto you." "God shall supply all .your need." We need not fear about not pleasing the world; Christ takes all excuses away. "Take no thought, saying, 'What shall we eat'? or 'what shall we drink' or 'wherewithal shall we be clothed?'... Take therefore no thought for the morrow; for the morrow shall take thought for the things of itself" (Matthew 6:31, 34). This is godliness, and godliness has the promise of this life as well as of that which is to come.

Thus we see that the Apostle's argument is based on the declaration of our Lord. We see that the only thing we can really glory in is the Cross of Christ, by which we are crucified to the world, because we are crucified with Christ, and this may mean perils and hardships. But there is a very important point connected with this matter—and it is, that it is a very personal and individual concern. The Apostle says, "I and Me." "I am crucified with Christ... He gave Himself for me" (Gal. 2. 20). This is the glory of the Gospel. The world talks about "man," and would deify "man "; but God, while he has condemned "man," saves "men." Men lose themselves in masses, and attempt to hide themselves in the multitude; but so soon as God speaks He separates one from the other, and deals with individual souls.

The Gospel does not deal with the masses as such; it takes out from the masses "a people for His Name." The Cross stands out in relation to all who are crucified with Christ. It is not that you have been born in a land where the Cross is honoured; it is not I that you have relations with a church that holds forth the Cross; it is not that you wear a cross, but that you are in living vital union with the crucified, so that you may say, "I have been crucified with Christ." Oh, what a wonderful expression! What a mysterious truth, when a lost sinner comes into the vital experience of it! Then for him these 1,800 years are blotted out, and he counts himself as being on Calvary in Christ.

So real is this great truth that the very crucifixion scene becomes part of our experience. In God's sight, in the Divine view, the saved sinner is identified with Christ Everything he gets from God is in Christ. He is "chosen in Christ," accepted in Christ, redeemed in Christ, and represented by Christ. Not only is this great fact and truth for every saved sinner, but in measure and in part the very experiences of Christ are ours. There is a sense in which they become true in our experience.

Rejection

Take, first, His rejection. He was "rejected of men," not rejected of the Father! No. We must make the distinction which the Scripture of truth makes. Not as is commonly said that the Father hid His face from the Son, but it was God against man. "Awake, O sword, against... the man that is My fellow" (Zechariah 13:7)—"against the man," not against "My Son." "The Son of Man" was "rejected of men," and the penitent soul, the sin-convicted sinner, has this experience. The first thought of such an one is, "I am accursed before God." Never before has the sinner known the terrible weight of Divine rejection till the Holy Law of the Holy God is written by the Holy Spirit on the fleshy tables of his heart. He that has been crucified with Christ enters into the real positions and in measure and in part into the experience of the darkness which overspread the heavens when Christ as man hung upon the cross, being made a curse for us The death due by the law is realised by such an one; conscience is now for the first time awakened; sin now for the first time is seen as that which separates from God; and the sinner loathes himself, as he thus enters into the first experience of what it is to be crucified with Christ.

Acceptance

But, secondly, there is, thank God, another experience. There is another view of the Cross of Christ, a Divine view, that of acceptance. If at His baptism and transfiguration the testimony of heaven was, "My beloved Son, in whom I am well pleased," surely it was so here when that Beloved One was accepted; for the holiness of God was then vindicated, the law of God was then honoured, the majesty of God was then magnified, and the same words are pronounced over every sinner who can say, "I have been crucified with Christ." The Father in heaven declares of Him and of every such an one, "My beloved son, in whom I am well pleased," and this, just because he is "accepted in the Beloved." Oh what a mighty reality there is in this great truth! How great the merits of this Saviour who has thus stood in the sinner's place, that the sinner might stand in His! No wonder that of all such the Holy Spirit has written, "There is now no condemnation to them that are in Christ Jesus." What a perfect satisfaction do we present! Who can measure the glorious answer to the law, the vindication of God's holiness, which the man (who a little while ago was a poor forlorn outcast sinner) brings before God, as soon as by grace he is enabled to say, "I have been crucified with Christ." Ah, this is light that will dissipate our darkness: all our bondage and fear would be instantly gone if we could only realize what it means to be "crucified with Christ."

His words become ours

But more than this is contained in the truth: not only Christ's acts and position are ours, but His words and utterances become in part ours. We know what it is to cry, "My God, my God, why has Thou forsaken me?" It is our cry of felt helplessness; it says, if God should cast us out for ever, "just and true is He." No reason can we find in ourselves, no ground for our acceptance can we find in our past living or present feelings. If saved at all, it must be by grace. and grace alone; and it shews that even this cry is the result of life which has been given; for though we cry, we say "My—my God." This is the beginning of the end, all else is assured when we can say my God. But the full measure of our absolute unworthiness is never experienced by us until this life and light has been imparted. It was when God said, "Let there be light," that ruin and desolation was seen at its worst, and so it is with the sinner. Talk not about repentance or contrition as a preparation for coming to Christ, for if we "have been crucified with Christ," we will surely experience the horror of this great darkness, but it will be coupled with hope. "My God."

Then another cry, "It is finished." What a blessed confession is this for Christ and for us! He who is crucified with Christ may take it upon his lips, and claim it as his own. His salvation is finished, the work is complete and perfect, nothing can be put to it nothing can be taken from it. Of course, if we mean to be saved by our own merits it will never be finished, and if we hesitate to say this, it is a proof that we are trusting to our own merits. If we are seeking to be saved by anything we can produce, our rest will always be unrest. But if saved by Christ, in Christ, with Christ, "for Christ's sake," then it is presumption if we do not admit to their fullest extent such statements as these, "He that believeth hath everlasting life," "is passed from death unto life," "shall not come into condemnation." It is not presumption to claim these words, but it is presumption, and unbelief too, if we hesitate as saved sinners to confess them. Come, all ye that are going about to establish your own righteousness, all ye that are seeking some other way to the glory of God, listen to this joyful sound of a finished salvation for all who have been crucified with Christ.

The world and the crucified

We cannot follow all the other thoughts which gather round "Christ Crucified," but there are two other facts that we must not omit. The Apostle says, "By whom the world is crucified to me, and I unto the world" (Galatians 6:14).

(1). What is the relation of the world to the crucified? Ah, it wore a very solemn aspect as the Crucified looked upon it, and he who is crucified with Christ sees it in the same way (in part and in measure). This is more than a figure. What did Paul mean when he said, "If ye be dead with Christ"—and "Ye are dead"? Not that we are actually dead, but judicially dead in God's sight, and therefore we are so to reckon ourselves. "If ye be dead with Christ," says the Apostle. "If ye then be risen with Christ, set your affections on things above, not on things on the earth, for ye are dead, and your life is hid with Christ in God" (Colossians 2:20; 3:1-3). What does this language imply? We are to be blind and deaf and indifferent to the world, as was Christ upon the cross. We are in the world, indeed, but rejected by it, not of it. All the hum and distracting noises fell upon unheeding ears, as they rose from Jerusalem and were wafted by the winds towards Calvary! If we are crucified with Christ we shall know something of this experience; only remember always that it is the effect and not the cause of being thus crucified. We cannot crucify our selves, we cannot make ourselves dead. How did the Lord Jesus pray? "I pray not that Thou shouldst take them out of the world, but that Thou shouldst keep them from the evil" (John 17:15). "Let me see life," says the man of the world, and he plunges into sin. "Let me see life," says the saved sinner, and he separates himself from sin. He only lives who is crucified and risen with Christ.

Joy and the crucified

(2). Those who are crucified with Christ know something of His sustaining joy. We are not left to imagine what this was, but we know that "For the joy that was set before Him He endured the cross, despising the shame" (Hebrews 12:2). Great were His sufferings, but greater still His joy. So it will be with us. This alone will support those who have been crucified with Christ. We shall never know the measure of His sorrow, but we shall know something of His joy. For a joy is set before us, and it will enable us to despise the shame and endure the suffering, and confess that "The sufferings of this present time are not worthy to be compared with the glory which shall be revealed in us" (Romans 8:18). "Our light affliction which is but for a moment worketh for us a far more exceeding and eternal weight of glory" (II Corinthians 4:17). Only those who have been crucified with Christ can truly say, "I live" (Galatians 2. 20), and I have the blessed hope of everlasting life. Can we say this? If we cannot, "What is our life?" Your life which you are living for yourselves? Let us not call this life. Let us not call our sinful pleasures joy. For what is our experience? Is it not a consciousness of a disappointed present, and a future without hope? Is it not a heart unsatisfied with earthly objects? Is it not a will at cross purposes with God's will? Do we call this *life*? Nay, call it what it is, *death*. Not dead with Christ, not dead to sin, but dead in *sins*.

May this testimony for the Crucified One quicken us together with Christ, that we may be able to say, "I have been crucified with Christ, nevertheless I live, yet not I, but Christ liveth in me; and the life which I now live in the flesh, I live by the faith of the Son of God, who loveth me, and gave Himself for me (Galatians 2:20).

"Abraham Believed God"

"For what saith the Scripture? 'Abraham believed God, and it was counted unto him for righteousness'" (Romans 4:3).

In these words we have the essence of the Gospel of God, and of His Grace. That Gospel is explained in Romans 1:1 to be the "Gospel of God." God's Good News; and faith cometh by hearing it. This is the Gospel that Abraham believed; he believed God; believed what God said. The patriarch's feet were firmly planted on God's ground; his eyes were fixed on God Himself. He had no shadow of doubt as to his possessing, in due time, all that God had promised. He did not hope it, still less did he doubt it, or go on asking for what God said He had given.

Oh! how few comparatively among the children of God really believe God, and without any reserve take this blessed ground of having died with Christ, of being risen with Christ, of being forgiven all sins, accepted in the Beloved, and sealed by the Holy Spirit! At times they hope it; when all goes smoothly with them they can venture to speak hopefully, but when things go against them, they feel the working of the old nature, and at once they begin to reason about themselves, and to question whether after all they are in reality the children of God. From such reasonings the passage to despondency and despair is an easy one.

All this is destructive to peace, because it is dishonouring to God. It is impossible to make progress in this condition. How can one run a race if he is not sure whether he has started? How can one erect a building if he has not laid the foundation? How can any one grow in grace if he is in doubt whether he has life, or has been "planted"? But some may ask, "How can I be sure about this? How may I know that I am saved?" The answer is, How do you know that you are a sinner and need saving? Is it because you feel you are one? Possibly so, but feeling is not a ground of faith; faith that is based on feeling is not a Divine faith at all. "Faith cometh by hearing." Faith must have respect to a promise not to a feeling. True faith rests on the testimony of God's Word. No doubt it is by the gracious energy of the Holy Spirit that any one can exercise this living faith, but we are speaking now of the true ground of faith, the authority for faith, the basis on which alone it can rest, and that surely is the Word of God, which is able to make wise unto salvation without any human intervention whatsoever.

Religion versus Christianity

There is scarcely a point on which Religion is more opposed to Christianity. Religion makes the word of God of none effect by its tradition and its superstition, and is thus in direct hostility to the truth of God. Religion has to do with the flesh; it admits that there is a Divine revelation; but it denies that anyone can understand it save by the interpretation of man; or, in other words, the Word of God is not sufficient without man's authority. God has spoken, but I am told I cannot hear His voice or understand His Word without; human intervention. This is Religion!

Infidelity, on the other hand, boldly denies a Revelation; it does not believe in such a thing. Infidels can write books, they can tell us their mind, but (so they say) God cannot! But where is the difference between denying that God has spoken, and maintaining that He cannot make us understand what He says? Both are alike dishonouring to God. Both deprive man of the priceless treasure of His Word. Both exalt the creature and blaspheme the Creator. Both alike shut out God, and rob the soul of the foundation of its faith.

This has ever been the device of the enemy, to quench the light of inspiration, to plunge the soul into the darkness of infidelity and superstition, to set aside the authority of the Word of God by any means in his power. He cares not by what agency he gains this end. Witness how he brought about the Fall by casting doubt on the Word of God. "Yea, hath God said?" It is therefore very important for us to seize this great fact which is brought out in our text, "Abraham believed God." Here was Divine faith. It was not a question of feeling or Religion. Indeed, if Abraham had been influenced by his feelings he would have been a doubter instead of a believer. For what had he in himself to build his faith on? "His own body now dead" (verse 19)? A poor ground surely on which to base a faith in the promise of an innumerable posterity. But we are told that "he considered not his own body now dead." What then did he consider? The Word of the living God, and on that he rested. This is faith.

Written for our sake

Mark what the Holy Spirit says of him. "He staggered not at the promise of God through unbelief... therefore it was imputed unto him for righteousness" (verses 20-22). Ah, but the anxious one may say, "What has all this to do with my case? I am not Abraham! I cannot expect a special revelation from God. How am I to know that God has spoken to me? How can I possess this precious faith?" Mark the answer to these questions in the Spirit's further words in verse 23. "Now it was not written for his sake alone that it was imputed to him, but for us also. if..." If what? If we feel it? If we realise it? If we experience anything in ourselves? Nay! But "if we believe on Him that raised up Jesus our Lord from the dead."

Oh! what solid comfort is here, what rich consolation! It assures the anxious one that he has the self-same ground and authority to rest upon that Abraham had, with much more light than Abraham had. For Abraham was called to believe God's Word as to what He promised, whereas we are privileged to believe in a fact which God has accomplished. He was called to look forward to something yet to be done; we look back at something that has been done, even an accomplished redemption attested by the fact of a risen and glorified Saviour, seated at the right hand of the Majesty on high.

But as to the ground or authority on which this faith is to be based, it is the same in our case as in that of Abraham—the Word of God. So it is written, "faith cometh by hearing, and hearing by the Word of God." There is no other foundation for faith but this; and the faith that rests on any other foundation is not true faith at all. A faith resting on human tradition, or on the authority of a Church, is not Divine faith; it is a mere superstition, it is a faith which stands in the wisdom of men, and not in the power of God (I Corinthians 2:5). It is impossible for us to overstate the value and the importance of this grand principle, the ground of a living faith. This is the Divine antidote to all the errors, evils, and hostile influences of the present day. There is a tremendous shaking going on around us, and it will grow worse. Minds are agitated; disturbing forces are abroad; foundations are being loosened; institutions are tottering; souls which found shelter in them are being dislodged and know not whither to turn. Confusion and judgment is written on all things ecclesiastical and political.

What do we need?

What is the one thing that we need? Simply this. A living faith in the living God! This is what is needed for all who are disturbed by what they see without, or feel within. Our unfailing resource is this, trust in a living God, and in His Son Jesus Christ, revealed by the Eternal Spirit in the Scriptures of Truth.

Here is the resting-place for faith. Here we solemnly exhort you to stay your whole souls. Here we have authority for all that we need to know, to believe, and to do. Is it a question of anxiety about your safety? Hear the Divine words, "Wherefore also it is contained in the Scriptures: Behold

I lay in Zion a Chief Corner Stone, elect, precious, and he that believeth on Him shall not be confounded" (I Peter 2:6). What solid comfort is here, what deep, settled repose! God has laid the foundation, and that foundation is nothing less than His own Eternal, co-equal Son. This foundation is sufficient to sustain all the counsels of God, to meet all the needs of the soul. Christ is God's own precious, tried, Chief Corner Stone. That blessed One who went down into death's dark waters; bore the heavy judgment and wrath of God against sin, and robbed death of its sting, and, having done this, was raised from the dead, was received up into Glory, and is now seated at the right hand of the Majesty in the Heavens. Such is God's foundation to which He graciously calls the attention of every one who really feels the need of something divinely solid on which to build, in view of the hollow and shadowy scenes of the world, and in prospect of the stern realities of the future.

God has spoken!

Dear reader, if this is your position, if you have come to this point, be assured that it is for you as positively and as distinctively as though you heard a voice from Heaven speaking to your own very self. In spite of sin in all its forms, and in all its consequences, in spite of Satan's power and Satan's malice, God has spoken! He has caused His voice to be heard in this dark and sinful world, and what has He said? "Behold, I lay in Zion... a foundation!" This is something entirely new! It is as though our blessed, loving and ever-gracious God had said to us, "Here I have begun anew, I have laid a foundation, and I pledge My word that whosoever commits himself to My foundation, whosoever rests in Mine Anointed, *i.e.*, in My Christ, whosoever is satisfied with My precious, tried, Chief Corner Stone, shall never, no never, no never, be confounded, never be put to shame, never be disappointed, never perish, world without end!" Oh, how blessed, how safe, how secure! If there were any question raised, any condition imposed, any barrier erected, you might well hesitate. If it were made a question of feeling, or experience, or of anything else that you could do, feel, be or produce, then you might justly pause, but there is absolutely nothing of the sort. There is the Christ of God, there is the Word of God, and what then? "He that believeth shall not he confounded."

In short, it is no more and no less than believing what God says, because He says it! It is committing your self to the word of Him that cannot lie. It is doing exactly what Abraham did. "Abraham believed God, and it was counted unto him for righteousness." It does not say Abraham understood God, because he did not; nor that Abraham believed something about God, but Abraham believed God, i.e., what He said. Thus he lived in peace with God, and died in the hope of Resurrection, of a Heavenly City, of a Heavenly Home. It is resting on the immovable rock of Holy Scripture, and thus proving the Divine and saving virtue of that which never failed any who trusted to it, never did, and never will, and never can. Oh! the unspeakable blessedness of having such a foundation in a world like this, where death and decay and change are stamped upon all, where friendship's fondest ties are snapped in a moment by death's rude hand, where all that seems (to nature's view) most stable is liable to be swept away in a moment by a popular Revolution, where there is absolutely nothing on which the heart can lean and say, "Now I have found permanent repose." Oh! what a mercy in such a scene to have a living faith in the living Word and in the written Word of the living God.

The soul that on Jesus has leaned for repose,
I will not, I will not desert to its foes;
That soul, though all hell should endeavour to shake,
I'll never, no never, no never forsake.

The Scope of a Passage May Best Be Discovered by Its Structure

INTRODUCTORY: THE HISTORY AND IMPORTANCE OF THE SUBJECT.

E very Word of God is pure; and His words, like all His works, are perfect. Perfect in order, perfect in truth, perfect in the use of number, perfect in structure.

"The works of Jehovah are great: sought out of all them that have pleasure therein" (Ps. 111:2).

Those who seek out His works find wondrous treasures; and see perfection, whether revealed by the telescope or the microscope. Neither of these exhaust those wonders. Both are only relative, and limited by human powers of sight.

It is the same with that most wonderful of all His works-His WORD. Use what powers of human intellect we may, we find that we know only "in part" (1 Cor. 13:9). Pursue any line of truth as far as our human minds can go, and we come to a wall of adamant, which we can neither mount over, pierce through, nor pass round; we return baffled, but solemnized by the fact that we know "in part."

We shall not be surprised therefore to find literary perfection as well as spiritual perfection. For there is perfection of literary form, as well as perfection of spiritual truth. The correspondence between parallel lines must always have been visible even on the surface to any one who carefully observed the Scriptures even as literary compositions. Josephus, Philo Judwus, Origen, Eusebius, Jerome, Isidore, among the Ancients, professed to have discovered metres in the Hebrew original. They were followed by others among modern scholars, some of whom agreed with them, while others refuted them.

In spite of Bishop Lowth's *Larger* and *Shorter Confutations*, which showed that all efforts to discover the rhymes and metres which characterize common poetry must be fruitless, some few writers have persevered in such attempts even to the present day. "Bishop Lowth was the first to put the whole subject on a better and surer foundation; reducing the chaos of mediaeval writings to something like order. His works were based on one or two who had preceded him, and had laid the foundations on which he built with such effect that he came to be universally recognised and appealed to as the ultimate and classical authority in these matters."[7]

But, as we have said, Bishop Lowth built on the foundations laid by others.

Abravanel, a learned Jew of the fifteenth century, and Azariah de Rossi[8] in the sixteenth century, were the first to demonstrate and illustrate the phenomena exhibited in the parallel lines of Holy Scripture. Azariah de Rossi published, in 1574-5, in Mantua, his celebrated work which he called *Meur Enayim*, or, *The Light of the Eyes*. It was a remarkable work and almost an encyclopedia of biblical literature in itself. Several of its chapters have been translated and published separately, in Latin and English. One chapter (ch. 9.) was sufficient to kindle Bishop Lowth's enthusiasm; and he translated it in his Preliminary Dissertation to his last great work, his translation of Isaiah (London, 1833). But, before this, Lowth had already used De Rossi's wonderful work to such purpose that in 1753 he published his *Praelections on the Sacred Poetry of the Hebrews*. This caused quite a sensation in the biblical world, and soon became of European fame.

Meanwhile Christian Schoettgen (born 187) had published in 1733-42 his Horce Hebraicce et Tatlmudicae (2 vols.), at Dresden and Leipzig; Bishop Lowth does not appear to have known of this work, for it anticipates him, and under the heading "Exergasia Sacra" it lays down the very doctrine which it remained for Lowth to improve and elucidate. Schoettgen lays down ten canons, and he illustrates each with three examples.

Bishop Jebb (born 1775 at Drogheda) published his *Sacred Literature* in London, 1820[9] and, until Thomas Boys began to write in 1824, Jebb's work had remained the last word on the subject. It was a review of Lowth's work and "an application of the principles so reviewed" to the illustration of the New Testament.

But both these works of Bishops Lowth and Jebb were almost entirely confined to the verbal correspondences in parallel lines; and never proceeded beyond short stanzas; and, even then, did not rise beyond what Lowth called "paralbelism" and Jebb called "Sacred Composition."

It was reserved for Thomas Boys to raise the whole subject on to a higher level altogether, and to lift it out of the literary parallelism be-

---

7. Rabbi Bon Isaac ben Jehudah, a celebrated Spanish-Jewish statesman, philosopher, theologian, and commentator, born 1437. His commentaries anticipate mach of what has been advanced as new by modern theologians (Kitto, Enc. Bib. article by C. D. G.).
8. Azariah de Rossi was born in Mantua, 1513.
9. Bishop Jebb, *Sacred Literature*, p. 15.

tween words and lines; and to develop it into the correspondence between the subject matter and truth of the Divine Word. In 1824 Thomas Boys soon followed up Bishop Jebb by publishing his Tactics Sacra, and in 1827-30 his Key to the Book of Psalms.[10]

While the successive works of Bishops Lowth and Jebb were enthusiastically and generally received, yet the works of Thomas Boys not only had to fight their way through much opposition, but are now practically unknown to Biblical students. Whether it is because they afford such a wonderful evidence of the supernatural and miraculous in the Bible, and such a proof of the Divine Authorship of the Word of God, that they are therefore the special object of attack by the enemies of that Word (both Satanic and human) He alone knows. But so it is.

Bishop Jebb, however, we are thankful to say, in the Second Edition of his Sacred Literature (1831), does recognize Boys's work in a note on page 74. He says, "Since the publication of Sacred Literature, this peculiarity of composition has been largely and happily illustrated, in his *Tactics Sacra*, by the Rev. Thomas Boys."

In 1851 Richard Baillie Roe made a great effort to revive the subject by publishing *An Analytical Arrangement of the Holy Scriptures* according to the principles developed under the name of Parallelism in the writings of Bishop Lowth, Bishop Jebb, and the Rev. Thomas Bobs.

This appears to have shared the same fate as all the others. Roe's book gives us too much as well as too little. It gives too much of dry analysis, and too little of the end for which it is made. Moreover, it is not improved by departing from Boys's simplicity; and serves only to complicate the subject by adding much that is arbitrary in arrangement. It may be said of Roe's method, that what is true is not new; and what is new is no improvement.

The facts being as thus stated, it shows that the subject has either not yet been grasped nor understood by Bible students; or, that it makes too much for the Inspiration and Divine Origin and Authority of the Word of God; and that there are spiritual powers, working with the human, whose one great object is to make the Word of God of none effect (Eph. 6:12 and 17).

---

10. This was only a description of his principles of Correspondence, which he applied to some sixteen Psalms. It was the privilege of Dr. Bullinger to edit Thomas Boys's manuscript; and, from pencilled notes in Boys's Interleaved Hebrew Bible (Boothroyd's Edition with Commentary, to complete and publish, in 1890, the whole of the Psalms with a Preface, and Memoir by his friend the Rev. Sydney Thelwall (who had been a personal friend of Boys), then Vicar of Westleigh, North Devon. An Introduction and Appendix were added by Dr. Bullinger as editor. This work was called *A Key to the Book of Psalms* to preserve a continuity with Boys's own title.

And yet, we may say that, no more powerful weapon has yet been placed in our hands outside that Word, which is "the Spirit's sword." It affords a wondrous proof of Inspiration; it gives us a clearer and more comprehensive view of the scope of the Scriptures, than the most learned and elaborate commentaries can ever hope to do; and it is capable of even turning the scale in doubtful, doctrinal, and critical questions.

By its means the student is led to views and truths, and reflections which, without it, would never have occurred to him. And it is not too much to say that until the Correspondences of the Biblical Structure are duly recognized we shall never get a correct translation or a true interpretation of many passages which are to this day dark and confused in both our Versions, the R. V. as well as in the AV Preaching on another subject, Bishop Lowth truthfully and feelingly observed that "It pleased God, in His unsearchable wisdom, to suffer the progress of the Reformation to be stopped mid-way; and the effects of it to be greatly weakened by many unhappy divisions among the reformed."[11]

The same may be said of the Law of Correspondence in the Structure of the Word of God, so wonderfully discovered and developed; and yet, needing to-day almost to be rediscovered, and certainly to be developed in its application to the whole Word of truth.

Parts of the world, remaining yet unexplored, are eagerly sought out without stint of labour or money. Would that the same zeal could be seen applied in the interest of this great subject.

THE PRINCIPLES GOVERNING THE STRUCTURE OF SCRIPTURE.

Having said thus much on the History and Importance of the Structure of Scripture, it is necessary that we should present an account and description of it in some kind of order more or less complete.

We do not propose to wade through all the Divisions and Subdivisions which have been suggested or laid down in connection with Parallelism as it relates to Lines. Our general object is to understand the Word of truth; and our special object is to consider how we may, by its means, arrive at the scope or subject of a particular passage.

The laws which govern this Parallelism of lines we will re-state as briefly as may be consistent with clearness. The main principles are as follows:

Parallel Lines are:

---

11. *Sermons and Remains of Robert Lowth*, D.D., p. 78.

(1) COGNATE[12] or GRADATIONAL, where the same thought is expressed in different or progressive terms: "Seek ye Jehovah, while He may be found; Call ye upon Him, while He is near." (Isaiah 55:6.)

(2) ANTITHETIC Or OPPOSITE, where the terms or subjects are set in contrast: "Faithful are the wounds of a friend; But deceitful are the kisses of an enemy." (Prov. 27:6.)

(3) SYNTHETIC, or CONSTRUCTIVE, where the terms or subjects correspond in a similar form of construction, either as equivalent or opposite. (As in Ps. 19:7-10. Isa. 44:28-28.) It discriminates and differentiates between the thoughts, as well as the words; building up truth by layers, as it were, placing one on the other.

> *"O the happiness of that man, Who bath not walked in the counsel of the ungodly; And bath not stood in the way of sinners; And bath not sat in the seat of the scornful." Psalm 1:1*

(4) INTROVERTED, where, whatever be the number of lines, the first line is parallel with the last; the second with the penultimate (or next to the last); the third with the antepenultimate (or next but one to the last); and so throughout, until we come to the two corresponding lines in the middle.

This was the discovery of Bishop Jebb; and could not be seen until a larger number of consecutive lines were examined.

> *"Make the heart of this people fat, And make their ears heavy, And shut their eyes Lest they see with their eyes, And hear with their ears And understand with their heart." Isaiah 6:10.*

Here, the correspondence is manifest.

It was, however, as we have said, reserved for Thomas Boys to lift the whole study out of the sphere of words and lines; and see the Law of Correspondence between subjects and subject-matter. Instead of occupying us with lines he bade us look at what he designated members. These members consisted of verses, and whole paragraphs. And the larger paragraphs were soon seen to have their own peculiar structure[13] or expansions.

This brings us to the consideration of what we have called the Structure of Scripture. Most of our readers will be acquainted with the practice of

---

12. This is Bishop Jebb's improvement of Bishop Lowth's word "synonymous", as including different as well as practically equivalent terms.

13. The reader will find further elucidation on this subject in *Figures of Speech*, by the same author.

marking their Bibles by ruling lines connecting the same word or words as they recur on the same or the adjoining page. The words recur, because the subject recurs; and the Law of Correspondences not only explains the practice of. such Bible markings, but shows why it can be done.

The principles and phenomena of the Laws of Correspondence are exceedingly simple, however perplexing they may appear to the eye at first sight. A little attention will soon make all clear to the mind as well as to the eye.

There are practically only two ways in which the subject is repeated:

1. By Alternation.
2. By Introversion.

1. Alternation.

This is where two (or more) subjects are repeated alternately.

(a) We call it Simple Alternation where there are only two subjects each of which is repeated in alternate lines. Thus

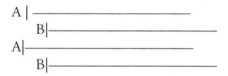

Here, the letters are used quite arbitrarily, and merely for the convenience of reference. Thus, the subject in the passage marked with an Italic letter (A) is the same as the subject in the passage marked with the corresponding Roman letter (A); while the B subject is the same as the B subject, the similar Roman and Italic letters indicating their similar, opposite and contrasted, or common subject.

(b) Where the two subjects are repeated more than once we call it Repeated Alternation, and indicate it thus

A1|————————————
   B1|————————————
A2|————————————
   B2|————————————
A3|————————————
   B3|————————————

And so on: all the members marked A corresponding in subject; and the members marked B corresponding in like manner.

There is no limit to this repetition. (c) Where there are more than two subjects alternating then we call it Extended Alternation; and there will be as many pairs, or sets of members, as there are subjects (unless, of course, these are repeated, when it would be a Repeated Extended Alternation):

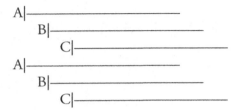

2. Introversion.

This is where the subjects are repeated, not in alternation, but in introversion; *i.e.* from opposite ends. In this case there will be as many subjects as there are pairs of introverted members. Suppose we have an example of four subjects. This will give us eight members, in which the 1st will correspond with the 8th; the 2nd with the 7th; the 3rd with the 6th; and the 4th with the 5th. Thus:

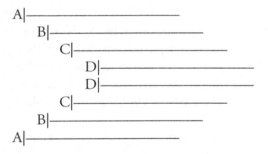

Now, with these few simple facts and phenomena, it is possible to have a very great variety. For they are practically unlimited, and can be combined in so many ways, and in such varying numbers, that there seems no end to the variety. But, all conform to the above simple laws, in which there is no exception.

EXAMPLES OF EACH PRINCIPLE.

We will give an example of each kind: premising (1) that 1- indicates the first part of a verse, -1 the latter part, and -1- a middle part; (2) that all the larger members have their own special Structures, in which the Correspondences of each may be expanded and exhibited. We give the examples from the Psalms because they are not encumbered with the human chapter divisions.

Simple Alternation.
Psalm 19.

A | 1-4-. The Heavens.
  B| -4, 6. In them "The Sun."
A| 7-10. The Scriptures.
  B| 11-14. In them "Thy Servant."

Repeated Alternation.
Psalm 145

A1| 1, 2. Praise promised. From me, to Jehovah Himself.
  B1| 3. Praise offered.
A2| 4-7. Praise promised. From others and me for Jehovah's works.
  B2| 8, 9. Praise offered.
A3| 10-12. Praise promised. From others, and His works,
      for Jehovah's kingdom.
  B3| 13-20. Praise offered.
A4| 21. Praise promised from me and others, to Jehovah Himself.

Introversion and Extended Alternation Combined.
Psalm 105.

A| 1-7. Exhortation to praise.
  B| 8-12. Basis of praise. Covenant in promise.
    C a |13. Their journeyings.. d ~17-22.
      b | 14, 15. Their prosperings
        c | 16. Their affliction
          d | 17-22 Mission of deliverance Joseph.
    C a | 23. Their journeyings.
      b | 24. Their prosperings.
        c | 25. Their affliction.
          d | 26-41. Mission of deliverance. Moses and Aaron
  B | 42-45-. Basis of praise. Covenant performed.
A | -45. Exhortation to praise.

In order to discover the structure of a particular passage it is necessary that we begin to read the portion of Scripture very carefully, and note the subject. We mark it A | -.

We read on until the subject changes, and we note and indent it thus B | -.

So far there can be no difficulty. But when we come to the next change we may find either a third subject, in which case we must further indent it and mark it C | -, or, we shall find the first subject again (as in Ps. 19 above). If it be the latter, then we know that we are going to find an alternation, (and this, either simple as in Ps. 19 above, or repeated as in Ps. 145 above), and we must mark it A |—and put it beneath the A | -. If it is a repetition of the second subject, then we know that it is going to be an Introversion, and must mark it B |—and place it under the B | -.

Let us take, as a working example, "The Prophecy of Zacharias," in Luke 1:68-79; this being a passage of Scripture complete in itself, and not a human or arbitrary division. We read verse 68 with the object of finding and noting its subjects: *"Blessed be the Lord God of Israel; for he hath visited and redeemed his people."* Here, the subject may be either "Visited "or "Redeemed. "So we give the place of honour to the former of these two words, and write it down, thus:

A | 68. Visitation.

We then read the next verse, "And hath raised up a horn, of salvation, for us in the house of his servant David." Here there can be no doubt that the subject is Salvation. This we must mark "B," and set it down, indented, thus

B 169. Salvation.

So far all is clear. But we know not, as yet, what the subject of the third member is to be. If it is Visitation we must set it down under "A "and mark it with an italic "A." Then we read slowly on:-"As he spake by the mouth of his holy prophets, which have been since the world began." It is manifest that we have, as yet, no repetition of either of the subjects in "A" or "B." If it had been that of "A," it would be a Simple or Repeated Alternation. If it had been that of "B," we should know that it was going to be an Introversion. But, it is a fresh subject, which is clearly, "Prophets." So we must mark it "C," and write it down, indenting it still more, thus

C | 70. Prophets.

Even now, there is nothing to tell us what the Structure is going to be. So far as we can see, it may be an Extended Alternation by the repetition of "A," "B," and "C "; or it may be an Introversion to be marked "C," "B," and "A." So we must read on:-" That we should be saved from our enemies, and from the hand of all that hate us." Here, we still have no Repetition,: but we find a new subject, which is clearly "Enemies."

So we must mark it "D," and write down (still further indenting it) thus:
D | 71. Enemies.

If the subject is a Repetition of any of the above subjects, we know that we are going to have an Alternation of some kind, or an Introversion. So we must still read on:-" To perform the mere promised to our fathers, and to remember his holy covenant." Here, there can be no doubt that we have again a new subject, and that it must be Covenant. So we put it down, as before, and still further indent it, thus

E | 72. The Covenant.

We can now be sure that we are going to have either a very Extended Alternation or an Introversion. So we must still read on, closely scanning every word, in order to get the clue. We find it in the next verse (v. 73):- "The oath which he sware to our father Abraham." Here, at length, we get one of our subjects repeated, as we were bound to do before long. It is the subject of "E," where the word "Covenant" is repeated in the synonymous word "Oath," thus indicating the sureness and certainty of the Covenant. We must mark this "E," and write it down under the "E," thus

E | 73. The Oath.

All we have to do now is to read on, and we soon discover that we have an Introversion, of great beauty, which we may now easily complete and set out, as follows Introversion.

The song of Zacharias (Luke 1:68-79).
A | 68. Visitation.
  B | 69. Salvation.
    C | 70. Prophets.
      D | 71. Enemies.
        E | 72. The Covenant.
        E | 73. The Oath.
      D | 74, 75. Enemies.
    C | 76. Prophet.
  B | 77. Salvation.
A | 78, 79. Visitation.

By practice and observation we shall soon surmount the initial difficulties; and in course of time the study and formation of structures will become increasingly easy and happy work. Advantages of Structure

THE ADVANTAGES AND IMPORTANCE OF THE STRUCTURES WILL BE SEEN

(a) In telling us what a particular passage of Scripture is all about. In other words, what is the Scope or the Subject of the passage we are studying.

(b) This will give us the key to the meaning which we are to put upon the words which are employed (as we saw under Canon L).

(c) In a case of doubt, the subject which is clearly stated in one of the members will inform us as to what it must be in the corresponding member, where it may not be so clearly stated.

(d) As the sense generally reads on from one member to its corresponding member, it will practically place the intervening member or members in a parenthesis. We shall therefore have to read on from "A" to "A" and from "B" to "B," etc., in order to get connected sense, instead of apparent confusion. This may be seen from any of the above examples, especially Psalm 105. But we may append another beautiful example

Hebrews 1., 2.
A | 1-2-. God speaking.
   B | 1:2-14. The Son. God. Better than Angels. '
A | 2:1-4. God speaking.
   B | 2:5-18. The Son. Man. Lower than Angels.

Here, ch. 2:1 ("A") reads on from 1:2- ("A"), and ch. 2:5 ("B ") reads on from ch. 1:14 ("B").

(e) Corroborative evidence is sometimes thus obtained for the support or otherwise of a various reading.

ILLUSTRATIONS OF THESE ADVANTAGES.

But the chief importance of this branch of our subject lies in the fact that the Structure gives us the Scope, and the Scope will give us the key to the meaning of the words.

It will be interesting if we now apply the principle involved in this our Second Canon to our First Canon, and to the same passages there considered. We shall thus see how the Structure of the passages which furnished the several illustrations under Canon I, does indeed give us their Scope: which, in turn, gives us the meanings of the words in 2 Pet.

1:20, 21 and 1 Pet. 3:18-20.

(a) "Private interpretation" (2 Pet. 1:20, 21). As the Epistles come to us as a whole, without division into chapters, we must not be guided by these human divisions at all in looking for the Structure; neither may we arbitrarily take a few verses, and say: these form a member by themselves. We mast show that these verses in question stand in their own special place and have their own proper correspondences in the Epistle as a whole. In looking, therefore, for the structure of 2 Pet. 1:20 we must first find the Structure of the whole Epistle, and see where this particular verse comes in; so that we may know of what subject it forms part; and with what other member it has its correspondence.

The 2nd Epistle of Peter as a whole.
(Combined Introversion and Extended Alternation.)
A | 1:1-4. Epistolary. Introduction. Grace and knowledge to be increased. Christ,. "God and Saviour."
  B | 1:5-11. Exhortations and Reasons.
    C | a | 1:12-15. Peter.
      b | 1:16-21. Apostles and prophets.
        c | 2. The wicked, etc.
    C | a | 3:1. Peter.
      b.| 3:2. Prophets and apostles.
        c | 3:3-13. The wicked, etc.
  B | 3:14-17. Exhortations and reasons.
A | 3:18. Epistolary. Conclusion. Grace and knowledge to be increased. Christ, "Lord and Saviour."

We thus see that ch. 1:20 forms part of a larger member (marked "b") which has for its subject "Apostles and prophets."

This one member (b, 1:16-21) is capable of a wonderful expansion, from which we see that it consists of two distinct parts: Apostolic witness (vv. 16-18); and, the Prophetic word (vv. 19-21).

These two, on careful examination, are seen to have a similar construction: Alternately negative and positive.

STUCTURES PART THREE
2 Peter 1:18-21.
(Simple Alternation Combined with Introversion.)
The Apostolic Witness (vv, 16-18).

b | D d | 1-16. *What it was NOT.* "Not cunningly devised (or self-originated) Myths."

    e | 1-16. *What it WAS.* A vision of the power and coining of Christ (Comp. Matt. 16:28, and 17:1-5). made known."

      E | 1-17, 18. *How it CAME.* Voice came from the excellent glory. Voice came from heaven. "Heard" and "made known."

D | e | 1-19. *What it IS.* A light to be well-heeded till the Day of Christ's coming shall dawn; and He, the Day Star, shall arise.

    d | 1- 20. *What it is NOT.* Not of its own reveal went. Not self-originating.

      E | 1-21. ***How it CAME***, *Not* brought *by the Will of Man*; but brought by pneuma hagion, or "power from on high." "Beard," and "spoken." The Prophetic Word (vv. 19-21).

From this we see the obvious contrast standing out very clearly between the self-originated myths that came by "the will of man"; and the Divine and heavenly Visions and revelations sent and received, and seen and heard from God in heaven.

This revelation is further seen to concern Christ's Coming. In "e" it is the Vision of it, as fore-shown in the Transfiguration: in "e" it is the grand reality of it, of which the Transfiguration was only a typical Vision. The former was believed on the Apostolic Witness: the latter was to be believed on the testimony of the *Prophetic Word*.

Further, the great subject, as to *How the Apostolic Witness* and the Prophetic Word came is strongly emphasized by the repetition of the same verb (phero), to *bring* or *bear*. We have it twice in each of the two corresponding members (E and E), showing us how the human *Witness* and the Divine Word were both. brought to us from heaven; and did not originate from any man or men on earth, as did the cunningly-devised myths.

It is this fact which stamps the Apostasy of the present day. Those who profess to be in the Apostolic succession turn away their ears from the prophetic Word; and, while they declare that many of its records are myths, are themselves "turned unto" the myths of man's devising.

We may add, in order to complete this passage, the following Expansions, verbatim

The Expansion of D
2 Peter 1:19, 20.
The Prophetic Word.

(Introversion-Six Members.)

D f | And we have more sure, the prophetic word (written prophecy);
    g | to which ye do well to take heed,
        h | as to a light shining in a dark place,
        h | until the day dawn, and the day star arise,
    g | in your hearts;
  f | this knowing first, that no prophecy of scripture came of its own disclosure.

Here, we observe, that the subject of "f" and "f" is the Prophecy. In "f" it is spoken of as a whole; in "f" "in part, a particular prophecy. In "g" and "g" we have Exhortation as to our duty with regard to it. In "g" we are exhorted to take heed to it; and in "g" how we are to take heed, *viz.*, in our hearts. Lastly, in "h" and "h" we have the Prophetic Word again. In "h" its character (a light in a dark place); and in "h" its duration and object (until the day dawn, *etc.*). Then in verse 21 we have the reason given.

The Expansion of E
2 Peter 1:21.
The Reason. (Introversion.)
E i | For not by the will of man
    k | was prophecy, at any time, borne in,
    k | but by the Holy Spirit, borne along,
  i | spake the holy men of God.

Here again we have in "i" and "i" man's relation to the Prophetic Word; in "i" negative, in "i" positive. While in "k" and "k" we have its origin; in "k'," negative, and in "k" positive. The above two Structures may be now explained by the following Key

THE KEY To D AND E.
The Prophetic Word.
2 Peter 1:19, 20.
(Introversion.)
D f | The prophetic word as a whole.
    g | Exhortation (general) to take heed to it.
        h | Its character: a light in a dark place.
        h | Its duration: until the Day dawn.
    g | Exhortation (particular): to take heed to it in our hearts.
  f | Prophecy in particular.

The Reason.

2 Peter 1:21.

(Introversion.)

E i | Man's part in it.

    k | How it did not come. } Negative.

    k | How it did come

  i | Man's part in it. } Positive.

Thus the scope, or great subject, of 2 Peter 1:16-21 is gathered from its structure; and it is seen to be, not what Scripture means, but whence it came: and it is concerned not with the interpretation of Scripture, but with its origin, as already shown above.

(b) "The spirits in prison " (1 Pet. 3:18-22). To understand this expression the Structure is necessary to give us the scope of 1 Pet.3.

Verse 19 does not stand by itself, but forms part of a larger member; and that member has its own Scope, or subject, which will give us the meaning of the expression—"The in-prison spirits."

This member is not to be arbitrarily delimited, but must be found from

The Structure of 1 Peter as a whole.

(Combined Introversion, and Extended Alternation.)

A | 1:1, 2. Epistolary.

  B | 1:3-12. Introduction. Giving out the great subject. "The End." Glory, after suffering for a season (*oligon*).

    C | a | 1:13-2:10. General Exhortations in view of "the End" 1:13). Grace to be brought at Revelation of Jesus Christ.

      b | 2:11-4:6. Particular Exhortations as to "sufferings" to be followed by "glory" (2:20; 3:17-22).

    C | a | 4:7-19. General Exhortations in view of "the End." Joy to be brought at Revelation of Christ's glory.

      b | 5:1-9. Particular Exhortations as to "sufferings" to be followed by "glory" (vs. 1).

  B | 5:10, 11. Conclusion. Embodying the great subject. "The End." Glory after suffering awhile (oligon).

A | 5:12-14. Epistolary.

From this structure it is perfectly clear that the Scope and subject of the whole Epistle is only one. This Scope is given in the words of I Peter 3:17.

"It is better to suffer for well doing than for evil doing."

This truth is enforced and illustrated and emphasized again and again throughout the Epistle. The verses which follow (3:17-4:6)' are added as the reason, which is given in proof of this statement of the Scope of this Epistle. The word "FOR" introduces it, and thus tells us that we have arrived at the very kernel of the whole Epistle. Not some passage which we are to explain as best we can and as though we wished it were not there: but which we are to embrace as all-important, and as though it were indispensable, as it is, to the subject of the Epistle.

But here again we must go back; for though we see that these verses (3:17-4:6) occur in the member "b," yet we see also that they form only a part of that member.

It is necessary for us, therefore, to go back, and see whether it is really an integral part, and whether the break in the whole member (2:11-4:6) really does occur at 3:17.

Expansion of "b"

1 Peter 2:11-4:8

(Extended Alternation.)

b D | 2:11. Exhortations (Personal).

    E | 2:12. Calumnies: and how to refute them.

        F | 2:13-3:7. Submission to man for the Lord's sake: "The will of God" (2:15). Reason: "For " (2:21), and Example of Christ in His sufferings.

  D | 3:8-15. Exhortations (General).

    E | 3:18. Calumnies: and how to refute them.

        F | 3:17-4:8. Submission to man for the Lord's sake: "The will of God" (3:17). Reason: "For" (3:18), and Example of Christ in His glorification.

The Correspondence of these members, each to each, is exceedingly exact and minute. From this we see that the last member F does actually commence with 3:17, the "For" corresponding exactly with the "For" in ch. 2:21: each "for" introducing the example of Christ.[14]

Now we are, at length, in a position to examine the further delimitation of this member F (3:17-4:6) which is as follows:

---

14. We cannot break off at end of ch.3 for ch.4 begins "Forasmuch then;" which shows that it follows in close continuation of ch. 3.

The Reasons for Submission to the Will of God
1 Peter 3:17-4:6
(Simple Alternation Combined with Introversion.)

F | G | c | 3:17. Reason for our suffering here, in the flesh, "if the will of
　　　　　　God be so."

　　　　d | 3:18-. Reason for Christ's suffering here as to His flesh, "put to
　　　　　　death:'

　　　　　　　　H | 3:18-22. Christ's glory which followed. (Resurrection,
　　　　　　　　　　Triumph, Glory, and Dominion).

　　G d | 4:1-. Reason for Christ's suffering here, in the flesh.

　　　　c | 1-5. Our suffering here in the flesh, at the "will of man," by "the
　　　　　　will of God." man," we shall

　　　　　　　　H | 4:6. Reason for our glory which shall follow. Though judged
　　　　　　　　　　in the flesh according to the "will of live again in resurrec-
　　　　　　　　　　tion according to the "will of God" (Compare v. 19).

Here we see the beautiful contrast between our suffering and Christ's; our glory and Christ's. This leads us up, naturally, to Christ's example, which follows verses 18-22, with which we are now concerned.

We see, from the above Structure, that these particular verses are located in the member "H," the subject of which is the Example of Christ in His glorification, corresponding with His example in ch. 2:21, which was Christ in His suffering.

In H (ch.3:18-22) the two examples are combined in order to connect the sufferings with the glory; and to show that Christ's glorious triumph which followed was the reason why it is better to suffer here, and now. (Compare ch. 3:18, with ch. 4:8.)

This is the triumph referred to in Col. 2:14, 15, where, having "spoiled principalities and powers, he made a show of them openly, triumphing over them in it."

The Triumph of Christ
H, 1 Peter 3:18-22
(Introversion and Extended Alternation.)

H | J | e | 3:18. The Resurrection of Christ.

　　　　f | 19. Result. (poreutheis), *having gone* (to Tartarus, 2 Pet. 2:4) He
　　　　　　made proclamation of His Triumph to the in-prison spirits

　　J | or angels.

g | 20 The insubjection of spirits in the days of Noah (Gen. 6. 2 Pet. 2:4. Jude 8).

     K | -20. Noah saved then. Ark the type. Material water the means.

     K | -21-. We saved now. Baptism the Antitype. Spiritual water the means.

J | e | -21. The Resurrection of Jesus Christ.

     f | 22-. Result. having gone into heaven, is on the right hand of God.

     g | 22. The subjection of angels, authorities, and powers.

Here we come to the direct proof that verses 18-22 have for their subject the "glory" of Christ, which followed on His "sufferings," forming the reason why "it is better to suffer for well-doing than for evil-doing." We see also the importance of the Structure in giving us the interpretation: for the "spirits "in verse 20 are shown to be "angels "in verse 22: the insubjection of the former being set in contrast with the latter. Thus we have another example of our second great principle that the scope, or subject, of a passage is to be sought for in its Structure. We have also some evidence as to the Divine origin of Scripture. For, these Structures are altogether beyond the power of "unlearned and ignorant men" such as Peter was (Acts 4:18), and are the best possible proofs we can have of Divine Inspiration.

STUCTURES PART FOUR

(c) *"Testament" and Covenant* (Heb. 9:15-28).-This will furnish us with an illustration of what we have already said on this passage above. There we have shown how the meaning of certain words in this passage is determined by its Scope. Now we have to show how the scope, and, therefore, the interpretation of the passage is determined by its Structure.

It is more profitable to show this in the case of passages we have already dealt with above, than to seek for other examples which would only divert our thoughts instead of concentrating them on the further elucidation of passages already in our minds.

When we say that Heb. 9:15-23 forms a distinct member by itself, the burden of proof devolves upon us; for, we may not make this arbitrary statement: we must show that it is so in fact, and that it has its own separate place in

The Epistle to the Hebrews as a whole.

(Introversion and Simple Alternation.)

A | i., ii. Doctrinal Introduction.

    B | 3:1-4. 13. The Mission of Christ.

        C | 4:14-16. General Application. "Having therefore") Boldness.

    B | 5:1-10. 18. The Priesthood of Christ.

        C | 10:19-12. 29. Particular Application. ("Having therefore")
        Boldness.

A | 13. Practical Conclusion.

We are now in a position to see where our particular passage (ch. 9:15-23) comes in. It is in the member marked B (ch. 5:1-10. 18) that we find it. We have to see, next, what particular part of that member it occupies, before we can discover its Scope.

Having thus given the Structure of the Epistle to the Hebrews as a whole, we are now in a position to see where the particular passage which we are considering comes in. We have before remarked that we cannot be guided in this matter by the chapter-breaks, which are entirely and only of human authority, which is no authority at all. In the case of an Epistle, we are compelled therefore to begin with the Epistle as a whole before we can discover the position of a particular passage or verse. The Structure of this member B, is based on the same model on which the Epistle itself, as a whole, is framed; and it is as follows:

The Priesthood of Christ

(B, Heb. 5:1-10. 18)

(Introversion, combined with Simple Alternation.)

B | a | 5:1-4. The Nature of Priesthood in General. (pas gar) "for every..."

    b | 5:5-10. Christ called by God after the order of Melchisedec.

        c | 5:11-6:20. Digression, concerning Melchi sedec as the Type.

    b | 7. Christ called by God after the order of Melchisedec.

        c | 8:1, 2. Summation, concerning Christ as the Antitype.

a | 8:3-10 18. The Efficacy of Christ's Priesthood inparticular. (*pas gar*)
    "for every..."

Now we see that the verses we are seeking (Heb. 9:15-23) farm part of a larger member, *viz.*, Heb. 8:3-10. 18, and that, in the above expansion, it is the member marked "a," which is the last member of the above Structure; and further, we see that its subject is the Efficacy and Superiority of Christ's Sacrifice as compared with the Priesthood of Aaron under the Law.

All we have to do now is to get the Scope of this member (a, ch. 8:3-10. 18) by observing its own special Structure.

We have said above that all these larger members have their own peculiar construction; but we must not be tempted nor turned aside from our main purpose; we must confine our attention, in each case, to the particular members involved in our search: and continue this until we narrow the whole question down to the passage we are examining, and are able to locate the verses (ch. 9:15-23) and thus discover their scope.

We are now in a position to do this by expanding the member "a." above, which we shall find to be as follows:

The Efficacy and Superiority of Christ's Priesthood.
(a, Heb, 8:3-10:18).
(Extended Alternation.)

a | d | 8:3-6. Christ's Priesthood. "A more excellent ministry," "a better covenant" on "better promises."

> e | 8:7-13. The Old and New Covenants compared and contrasted.

>> f | 9:1-5. The Earthly Sanctuary a copy of the Heavenly Pattern,

>>> g | 9:6-10. The Offerings.

> d | 9:11-14. Christ's Priesthood. "A greater and more perfect Tabernacle." "His own blood."

>> e | 9:15-23. The Old and New Covenants compared and contrasted.

>>> f | 9:24. The Heavenly Sanctuary the pattern of the Earthly Copy.

>>>> g | 9:25-10. 18. The Offerings.

Here we see that our special member which we are tracking out is found in that marked "e," ch.9:15-23. Thus, at length, we learn that its subject is The Old and New Covenants Compared and Contrasted. This settles its Scope for us. All that remains for us to do now is to confirm it by discovering its own Structure and seeing whether this be really the case. To see the full force of this it will be well to look also at the member with which it stands in Correspondence, *viz.*, "e," ch. 8:7-13, which is an Introversion. It also follows the model of the Epistle as a whole.

The Old and New Covenants Compared and Contrasted.
(e, Heb, 8:7-13.)

(Introversion and Simple Alternation.)

e | h | 7, 8. The First Covenant Faulty.

     i | 9. The New Covenant (Negative). Not the same in the making and material.

        k | 10. The New Covenant (Positive). Spiritual.

     i | 11. The New Covenant (Negative). Not the same in its result and effect.

        k | 12. The New Covenant (Positive). Spiritual,

   h |13. The First Covenant Evanescent.

Now we are in a position to look at the member with which we are specially concerned, and again we notice that the Structure follows the model of the Epistle as a whole:

The Old and New Covenants Compared and Contrasted,
(e, Heb, 9:15-23,)

(Introversion and Simple Alternation.)

e | L | 9:15. The Old Covenant related only to "the promise of the eternal inheritance."

     m | 16. Death necessary for its making.

        n |17. Reason for this necessity.

     m | 18. Blood necessary for its consecration. n | 19-23-. Reason for this necessity.

   L | 23. The New Covenant related to "the heavenly things themselves."

It is impossible to miss the great subject of these verses It forbids us to ignore its importance, which is so essential to the whole argument. To arbitrarily change this subject is to entirely miss its scope, and to be driven to force a meaning into the words and expressions which are quite foreign to their Biblical usage.

(d) "Absent from the Body."-2 Cor. 5, will furnish us with another illustration of the importance of the Structure in determining the Scope. And we have seen, under Canon L, the necessity of the Scope to give us the meaning of the word, and to show us how indispensable it is for a right understanding of the whole.

The Structure will show us how much we lose by the break between the fourth and fifth chapters of the second Epistle to the Corinthians. Chapter

5 commences as though it began an entirely fresh subject, whereas it begins with the word "FOR," which shows that it is the conclusion of what had been begun towards the end of ch. 4. That subject is Resurrection as our blessed hope in view of the perishing of our outward man day by day. As a comforting conclusion it is added, "FOR we know that if our earthly house of this tabernacle were dissolved, we have a building of God, an horse not made with hands, eternal, in the heavens." This is one of the "things unseen," and which are "eternal"; at which, and for which, we are to "look."

Where the real literary and logical breaks occur can be discovered only from the Structure. As a matter of fact, 2 Cor. 5. forms part of a member which runs from 2 Cor. 3. 1-6. 10; but we must not make such an arbitrary statement without producing the evidence, so that others may judge for themselves as to its accuracy. To prove this we must first give

The Structure of 2 Cor, as a whole.
A | 1:1, 2. Salutation.
  B | a | 1:3-11. Thanksgiving.
      b | 1:12. Paul's Ministry.
          C | 1:13-2:13. Epistolary.
  B | a | 2:14-17. Thanksgiving.
      b | 3:1-6. 10. Paul's Ministry.
          C | 6:11-13. 10. Epistolary.
A | 8:11-14. Salutations.

Without going into the exquisite beauties of C and C,' we note that the small portion in which the expression "Absent from the body" occurs is the member marked b (ch.3:1-6.. 10). We must dissect and expand this member, which will be seen to be as follows

The Character of Paul's Ministry.
(b, 2 Cor. 3:1-6. 10.)
b | c | 3:1-3. Commendation (Positive)
    d | 3:4, 5. Trust in God. God's Sufficiency.
        e | 3:.6-18. The Ministry of the New Covenant.
            f | 4:1-5. 11. Support under Afflictions.
  c | 5:12, 13. Commendation (Negative)
    d | 5:14-18-. Love of Christ. All of God.
        e | 5:18-6:2. The Ministry of Reconciliation.
            f | 6:3-10. Approval under Afflictions.

We are thus narrowing down the issue, which is now seen to lie in the member marked "f" (ch. 4:1-5:11). The subject of this member is Support under afflictions; and its Structure is a repeated alternation, as follows:

Support under Afflictions.
(2 Cor. 4:1-5. 11.)

f | g1 | 4:1-6. Confidence (Neg.). "We faint not."

     h1 | 4:7-15. Grounds. "Earthen vessels." The working of death in them (4:12), with pledge of Resurrection (4:14).

  g2 | 4:16-. Confidence (Neg.). "We faint not."

     h2 | 4:16-5:5. Grounds. "Earthly house." The working of afflictions (4:17), and the working of God, in Resurrection (5:5).

  g3 | 5:6-11 Confidence (Pos.). "We are confident."

We need not pursue these expansions further, though we might well do so. We can see very clearly now, that the wonderful ground of support of Paul and Timothy in their afflictions was the consideration of the "unseen" things, as outweighing the "things seen"; so that though the "earthen vessels" of their bodies were dissolved there was the "excellency of the power" of God which would be put forth in Resurrection.

It is thus seen how the break between chapters iv. and v. destroys the connection: in fact, breaks in two the one member, "ha" (ch. 4:16 -5:5), which has only one subject, *viz.*, Resurrection, as the ground of the confidence, and the reason for not fainting in their labours of ministry.

We might have included this under the head of rightly dividing the Word of truth as to its literary form, as shown by the division into chapters. We might also have included it under the heading of the importance of the Scope of a passage (Canon L). We might have included it under the heading of the importance of the Context (see below, Canon III.). It belongs to all three; but considering that the Structure is necessary to the crowning proof, we have given this illustration here.

It is little less than a crime for anyone to pick out certain words and frame them into a sentence, not only disregarding the Scope and the context, but ignoring the other words in the verse, and quote the words "absent from the body present with the Lord" with the view of dispensing with the hope of Resurrection (which is the subject of the whole passage), as though it were unnecessary; and as though "presence with the Lord" is obtainable without it.

Apart from the doctrine involved, and apart from the teaching of Tradition (true or false), it is a literary fraud thus to treat words which the Holy Ghost teacheth. We see therefore, for it must be clear to us, that the Scope of a passage is the key to its words; and that the Structure of a passage is the key to its Scope. This will show us the importance of our second Canon. How great must be our loss if we fail to use this key to the wonderful words of God. Like all His works they bear the minutest searching out.

All the works of God are perfect. And the microscope and telescope can both be used to examine them; though neither of them can ever exhaust the wonders of God's works. In both directions an increase of the power of the lens will reveal new beauties and fresh marvels. the The Word of God, being one of His works, must have the same phenomena: and nothing exhibits these phenomena like the Study of its Literary Structure. To us, God's Word is the greatest and most important of all His works. If we understand all His other works (which no one does or can) and yet know not His Word, our knowledge will not carry us beyond the grave.

But we must not lose sight of the great underlying lesson, and the great outcome of the whole of this subject, which is this: If the external form be so perfect, what must the inward truth be: if the setting be so valuable, how valuable must be the jewel: if the literary order be Divine, how solemn must be the warnings, how important the truth, how faithful the promises, how sure the words of which the Word is made up.

Right Division

The one great requirement of the Word is grounded on the fact that it is "the Word of truth." And this fact is so stated as to imply that, unless the Word is thus rightly divided we shall not get "truth"; and that we shall get its truth only in proportion to the measure in which we divide it rightly. The Requirement is thus stated in II Tim. 2:15: "Give diligence to present thyself approved to God, a workman having no cause to be ashamed rightly dividing the word of truth."

The word in question here orthotomounta. As this word occurs in no Greek writer, or even elsewhere in the New Testament, we can get little or no help from outside, and are confined to Biblical usage.

It is used twice in the Septuagint for the Hebrew *vashar*, to be right, or straight. In Prov. 3:6; 11:5, the Hebrew is *Piel* ,to make right (as in II Chron. 23:30; Prov. 15:21; Isa. 40:3; 45:2,13). But it is the Greek word that we have to do with here, in II Tim. 2:15; and we cannot get away from the fact that *temno* means to cut; or, from the fact that we cannot cut without dividing. To divide belongs to the very nature of the act of cutting. Even as applied to directing one's way it implies that we divide off one way from others—because we desire to follow the right way and avoid the wrong.

The only Biblical guide we have to the usage of the word is in Prov. 3:6, "In all thy ways acknowledge him And he shall direct thy paths." In the margin the R.V. gives, "make straight or plain" as an alternative rendering for "direct." But our ways can only be made straight or plain by God's causing us to proceed on our Way aright—*i.e.*, by avoiding all the ways that are wrong, and going in the one way that is right; in other words, the right way is divided off from all the wrong ways.

What else can the word mean in II Tim. 2:15? It matters little what others have thought or said. We could fill a page with their names and their views, but we should learn but little and only become confused. The duties of Priests, Furriers, and Ploughmen have been referred to as indicating the correct meaning. But we need not leave the Biblical usage, which associates the word with guidance in the right way.

> *The scope of the verse plainly teaches that:*
> *Our one great study is to seek God's approval, and not man's.*
> *We are to show all diligence in pursuing this study.*
> *As workmen, our aim is to have no cause to be ashamed of our work.*
> *In order to gain God's approval and avert our own shame we must rightly*
> *   divide the word of truth.*

To do this we must direct our studies in the right way.
This great requirement is associated with the Word in its special character
as being the Word of truth; i.e., "the true Word."

All this tells us that we shall not get the truth if we do not thus rightly divide it; and that we shall get the truth only in proportion to our "rightly dividing" it.

Other titles of the Word have their own special requirements. As "the engrafted Word" it must be received with meekness (Jas. 1:21). As "the Faithful Word" we must hold it fast (Tit. 1:9). As "the Word of life" we must hold it forth (Phil. 2:16). But, because this is "the Word of truth," its paths must be well noted, the sign-posts must be observed, the directions and guides which are in the Word itself must be followed. We are to "give diligence" to this great Requirement of the Word just because it is "the Word of truth."

Rightly dividing the Word as to its Subject Matter

It is the common belief that every part of the Bible is to be interpreted directly as referring to the Church of God; or as pertaining to every person, at every stage of the world's history. This neglect of the precept to rightly divide it is an effectual bar to the right understanding of it, and to our enjoyment in its study. This non-understanding of the Word is the explanation of its neglect, and this neglect is the reason why so many who should be feeding on the spiritual food of the Word are so ill-fed in themselves; and so ill-furnished for every good work (II Tim. 3:17). While the Word of God is written for all persons, and for all time, yet it is as true that not every part of it is addressed to all persons or about all persons in all time.

Three distinct classes of persons

Every word is "written for our learning," and contains what all ought to know: yet, its subject- matter is written according to the principle involved in I Cor. 10:32, and is written concerning one or other of three distinct classes of persons:

"The Jews, The Gentiles, and The Church of God."

According to the general belief, everything that goes to make up the subject-matter of the Word of God is about only one of these three: and, whatever may be said about the other two (the Jews and the Gentiles), all is to be interpreted of only the one, viz., the Church of God. This comes of that inbred selfishness which pertains to human nature: which, doing with this as with all beside, is ever ready to appropriate that which belongs to others. But no greater impediment to a right understanding of the Word could possibly be devised.

We are quite aware that, in saying this, we lay ourselves open to the charge which has been made by some, that we are "robbing them of their Bible." But the charge is groundless; and it arises from a total misapprehension of what we mean, or from a perversion of what we have said. It is necessary, therefore, for us to repeat, and to state categorically our belief that every word from Genesis to Revelation is written for the Church of God. There is not one word that we can do without: not one word that we can dispense with, without loss. We deprive no one of any portion of the Word of Truth. We protest against robbery in this sphere, as in all others. It is not we who rob the Church of God; but it is they who rob the Jews and the Gentiles. We would fain restore stolen property to the rightful owners; property which has been stolen by the very persons who charge us with robbery! We may indeed retort in the words of Rom. 2:21: "Thou that preachest a man should not steal, Dost thou steal? "We are prepared to make this counter-charge, and to sustain it. The charge against us we disclaim; while those who make it are themselves guilty of the very offence for which they condemn us.

We hold that what is written to and about the Jew, belongs to and must be interpreted of the Jew. We hold that what is written of and about the Gentile; belongs to and must be interpreted of the Gentile. We hold that what is written to and about the Church of God, belongs to and must be interpreted of the Church of God. Is this robbery? or, Is it justice? Is it stealing? or, Is it restitution?

Evidence of the misappropriation (to use a milder term) is furnished by the Bible which lies open before us. In speaking of the page-headings of Isa. 29 and 30, in our current editions of the English Bibles (KJV), in which the former is declared to be "Judgment upon Jerusalem"; and the latter, "God's mercies to his church." . What is this but not only wrongly dividing the Word of truth, but the introduction of error, by robbing Jerusalem of her promised "mercies" and appropriating these stolen mercies to the Church? while the "judgments" are left for Jerusalem, just as burglars take away what is portable, and leave behind what they do not want or cannot carry away.

We believe God when He says that the Visions shown to Isaiah were "concerning Judah and Jerusalem" (Isa. 1:1). True, they were written for us; and "for our learning" (Rom. 15:4); but they are not addressed to us, or written concerning us, but "concerning Judah and Jerusalem." It would be an act of dishonesty, therefore, for us thus to appropriate, by interpreting of ourselves, that which was spoken of Israel. In like manner, if we take, as some do, the words of the Epistle to the Ephesians as though they were written to or concerning the Gentiles (or the unconverted world), then we not only rob the Church of God of its most precious heritage, but we teach the "Universal Fatherhood of God" instead of His Fatherhood of only those who are His children in Christ Jesus. It will thus be seen that unless we rightly divide the subject-matter of the Word of truth we shall not get the truth, but shall get error instead.

Every part of the Bible is written "concerning" one or other of these three divisions, or classes of persons. Sometimes in the same passage or book there may be that which is concerning all three. Sometimes a whole book may be concerning only one of these three, and the other two be altogether excluded. We may all three learn much from what is written of only the one; for the inspired, God-breathed Word is "profitable for doctrine, for reproof, for correction, for instruction," for all who shall read it (II Tim. 3:16). That which happened to Israel happened unto them for ensamples; "and they are written for our admonition " (1 Cor. 10:11). "Whatsoever was written aforetime was written for our learning" (Rom. 15:4).

But while this is so, and remains true; what we mean is that every Scripture is written concerning one or other of these three classes; and is especially addressed to that particular class. This class has therefore the prior claim to that Scripture. The interpretation of it belongs to that class; while the other two may apply it to themselves, and are to learn from it. But, inasmuch as it is only an application and not the interpretation, such application must be made only so far as it agrees with the interpretation of those Scriptures which are specially addressed to and relate to such class. Otherwise we shall find ourselves using one truth to upset another truth; we shall be setting what is true of one class in opposition to what is true of another class. All that we are concerned with now is the right dividing of the subject-matter of the Bible, which is three-fold. And the great requirement of the Word as to this is, that we should, and must, whenever we study any portion of the Word of God, ask the question, "Concerning whom is this written?"

Whichever of the three it may be, we must be careful to confine and limit the interpretation of that passage to the class whom it concerns; while we may make any application of it to ourselves so long as it does not conflict with what is written elsewhere concerning "the church of God."

We must not take that which concerns the Jew and interpret it of the Church. We must not take that which concerns the Church and interpret it of the world. We must not take what is said concerning the Gentile and interpret it of the Church. If we do, we shall get darkness instead of light, confusion instead of instruction, trouble instead of peace, and error instead of truth.

The Christian's Greatest Need

There is one thing that the Christian needs more than he needs any other thing. One thing on which all others rest; and on which all others turn. It is certain from the Word of God, and also from our own experience, that "we know not what we should pray for as we ought". But "the Spirit Himself helpeth our infirmities" (Romans 8:26). He knoweth what we should pray for. He knoweth what we need. He maketh intercession for us and in us. He teacheth us how to pray, and in Ephesians 1:17, we have His prayer set forth in these words: "that the God of our Lord Jesus Christ, the Father of glory, may give unto you the spirit of wisdom and revelation in the knowledge of him."

This, then, must be our greatest need: *A true knowledge of God.*

If the Holy Spirit thus puts it before all other things, it must be because it is more important than any other thing; yea, than all others put together. This, it is, that lies at the foundation of the Christian Faith; at the threshold of Christian life. It is the essence of all trust. We cannot trust a person if we do not know him. At least, it is safer for us not to do so; and as a rule we do not.

But on the other hand, when we know a person thoroughly well, we cannot help trusting him!. No effort to trust is required when we perfectly know a person. The difficulty then is, not to trust. Why, then, do we not thus trust God? Is not the answer clear? It is because we do not know Him! Thus we see how this knowledge of God is our greatest need; the very first step of our Christian course. Our trust will ever be in proportion to our knowledge.

If we knew, for example, a billionth part of God's infinite wisdom, we should see our own to be such utter folly, that we should not merely be "willing" for His will, but we should desire it. It would be our greatest happiness for Him to do and arrange all for us. We should say, "Lord, I am so foolish and ignorant; I know nothing, and can do nothing; I can see only this present moment; I know nothing of to-morrow. But Thou canst see the end from the beginning. Thy wisdom is infinite, and thy love is infinite; for, our Saviour and Lord could say of us to Thee, as Thy beloved Son—"Thou hast loved them, as thou has loved me" (John 17:23). Do, then, Thine own will. This is my desire, the desire of my heart. This is what I long for above 'all things.'" This is far beyond being "willing". We may be willing for a thing, because we cannot help it. It may be even a low form of Christian fatalism. A Mahommedan may be thus resigned to the will his god.

But what we are speaking of is far, far beyond the modern gospel of holiness; far in advance of merely being "willing". Those who are in the still lower condition; not "willing," but "willing to be made willing," do not see that this condition arises from not knowing God; not knowing how infinite is His love, how vast is His wisdom, how blessed and how sweet is His will. If they did but know something of this, they would yearn for His will. It would be the one great earnest desire and longing of their hearts for Him to do exactly what is pleasing in His own sight, in us, and for us, and through us.

Not knowing this secret, Christians, everywhere, are striving and labouring to be "willing" by looking at themselves; and by some definite "act of faith" to do something of themselves. Instead of thinking of His wisdom and His love, they are thinking of themselves and of their "surrender".

But this is labour in vain. Even if it should seem to accomplish something, it is only like tying paper flowers on a plant. They may look natural and fair; but they have no scent, and no life; no fruit, and no seed. It is an artificial, fictitious attempt to produce that which, if they did but know God, would come of itself, without an effort: yea, the effort would be to stop or hinder the mighty power of a true knowledge of God.

The trouble with us is, if we prove our hearts to their depth, that, at the bottom, we think we know better. We would not say it for the world, we would hardly admit it to ourselves. But there it is; and the difficulty of being "made willing" is the proof of it.

If we really knew Him, and believed that He knows better than we do what is good for us, there would be no effort whatever, but only a blessed irrepressible desire for His will.

Before we proceed further to consider some other of the practical effects of this knowledge, let us notice the fact that there are two words in the original for this knowledge of God, two verbs which mean to know. As these are used some times in the very same verse, it is very important that we should carefully distinguish that which the Holy Spirit has so especially emphasised. There are, indeed, six Greek words which are translated to know, but these two are the most common.

1. The one, *oida*, means to know without learning or effort; and refers to what we know intuitively, or as a matter of fact or history.

2. The other, *ginosko*, means to get to know; by effort, or experience, or learning.

Practical Christian living

The importance of getting to know God is our one great need. This knowledge is not only the basis of trust in God; not only the foundation of Christian faith; but of Christian life. Practical Christian life and walk will be in direct proportion to our knowledge of God.

Look at Colossians 1:9,10, where we have the practical outcome of the prayer in Ephesians 1:17. In Ephesians 1:17 we have the prayer itself. In Colossians 1:9,10, we have it applied for our correction and instruction. Carefully weigh the words. "For this cause, we also, since the day we heard it, do not cease to pray for you, and to desire"—Desire what? "that ye might be filled with the knowledge (the noun from No. 2, i.e., acquired knowledge) of his will in all wisdom and spiritual understanding." Why? For what purpose? To what end? "That ye may walk worthy of the Lord unto all pleasing, being fruitful in every good work, and increasing in the knowledge of God."

Then, to walk worthy of the Lord, I must know Him? Exactly so. If I would please Him in all things I must know what will please Him. Is this all that is required? All that I have to do? Yes, this is all. Then I have not to rush hither and thither; from Convention to Convention? No, I have to sit down before God's Word, and get to know Him through that. There is no other way of getting to know Him. And He has given us His Word, and revealed Himself therein, on purpose that we may study it and find out what it is that pleases Him; what it is He loves; what it is He hates; what it is He does. To get to know His wisdom, His will, His infinite love, His almighty power, His faithfulness, His holiness, His righteousness, His truth, His goodness and mercy, His long-suffering, His gentleness, His care, and all the innumerable attributes of our great and glorious God.

See how this knowledge is absolutely necessary, if we would please God. We cannot please any of our friends unless we know what they are pleased with. If we would make a present to one of them, we naturally think, or try to find out, what it is he or she needs or would be pleased to have. If we are receiving a guest, we naturally try to remember or find out what pleases him in food or drink, in occupation or recreation. If we cannot find this out, then we have to guess at it, and we may or may not succeed in our effort to please. We may take the greatest trouble and pains, and yet, after all, we may arrange for or provide the very thing which is most disliked. It is even so with our God.

Where can we go?

How are we to find out the things that please Him? How are we to discover the things He approves?

Only from His Word.

There, and there alone can we get to know Him. There alone shall we learn the fullness of the Spirit's prayer for us in Ephesians 1:17; and the blessed practical outcome of it in Colossians 1:9,10.

No man has this knowledge of God intuitively. No minister can even help in imparting it, except in and by the ministry of that Word. His own thoughts are valueless. Only so far as he enables us to understand that Word can he be of any assistance to us. He may be mistaken himself, and very easily be a hindrance instead of a help. God has revealed Himself in His written Word, the Scriptures of truth; and in the Living Word His Son, Jesus Christ. And it is by the Communicated Word revealed in our hearts by the Holy Ghost that we begin thus to get to know Him, whom to know is Life Eternal.

This is the one great reason why the written Word is given to us. It is not given merely as a book of general information, or of reference; but it is given to make known the invisible God. Why do we read it? Why do we open it at all? What is, or ought to be, our object in reading it? Do we read a portion that someone else has selected for us? Do we read that portion because we have promised someone we would do so? Or do we open it, and sit down before it with the one dominant object to find out God; to discover His mind; to get to know His will.

Those who are not thus engaged make their own god out of their own thoughts and imaginations. They have to fall back on what they think their god likes!

Thousands make their gods with their hands, out of wood, or stone, or bread. Thousands more make him out of their own heads. But, being ignorant of God's Word, they are alike ignorant of the God Who has there revealed Himself.

We must worship Him in spirit

See the power of this truth as it is applied to what is called "Public Worship" or "Divine Service". How many still worship "the unknown God", and serve themselves; and do what is pleasing in their own eyes, studying only their own tastes! Ignorant of that great rubric, John 4:24, "God is a Spirit, and they that worship Him must worship Him in spirit and in truth" (*i.e.*, truly in spirit), they talk of the kind of service they prefer, and say, "I don't like that at all"; or, "I do like that so much"; as though "places of worship," so-called, were opened merely for persons to go in and do what pleases themselves, forgetful of that word "must," which dominates the whole sphere of what we call worship.

Worship "must" be only with the spirit. We cannot worship God—who is a Spirit—with our eyes, by looking on at what is being done. We cannot worship God with our noses, by smelling incense, whether ceremonially or otherwise used. We cannot worship God with our ears, by listening to music, however well it may be "rendered". No! worship cannot be with any of our senses; or by all of them put together. It must be spiritual, and not sensual. The worshippers must be spiritual worshippers, for "the Father seeketh such to worship Him" (John 4:23).

How many of such worshippers frequent our churches and chapels? How many are still worshipping "the unknown God" (Acts 17:23)?

Is it possible that, if the true God were known—the great, the High and Holy God, who dwelleth not in temples made with hands; the God who inhabiteth eternity; the God in whose sight the very heavens are not clean, and who chargeth His angels with folly—is it possible, we ask, that any who know Him could imagine, for one moment, that He "seeks" or could be pleased with, or accept, or regard a congregation turning the Bible into "a book of the words," and listening, for example, to a girl singing a solo, getting as high a note as she can, and holding it out as long as she can! Is that what The Great and Infinite God is seeking? Is that the occupation of the heart with Himself which He says He "must" have? No indeed! and the greater the ignorance of God, the deeper and more degraded will become the accompaniments of what is called "Public Worship".

A true knowledge of Christ

So far we have spoken only of a knowledge of God—the Father. But it is also of the greatest importance that we should have a true knowledge of Christ.

This is the Christian's one object, as well as his greatest need.

This is set forth with remarkable clearness and force in Philippians 3. In the ninth verse we have our standing in Christ expressed in the words

"Found in Him."

This is explained as not having our own righteousness, but that which is through the faith of Christ; "the righteousness which is of God by faith".

Clothed in this righteousness, nothing of self is seen by God. Like the stones in the Temple, they were covered over first with cedar-wood; and the cedar-wood was covered over with gold. Then it is added, "there was no stone seen". These words are not necessary either for the grammar, or for the sense; for how could the stone be seen if thus doubly covered up? No! the words are graciously added to emphasize the antitype, and to impress upon us the blessed fact that, when covered with Christ's righteousness there is nothing of self seen in our standing before God. We are already "in the heavenlies, in Christ"; and are comely in all His comeliness, perfect in all His perfection, accepted in all His merit, righteous as He is righteousness; yea, holy as He is holy, and loved as He is beloved. All this is included in those words, "found in Him". And being thus "found in Him" for our standing, we have in verses 20, 21 our hope; which, is to be *Like Him* in resurrection and ascension glory at His coming. Hence "we look for the Saviour, the Lord Jesus Christ: who shall change our vile body, that it may be fashioned like unto his glorious body, according to the working whereby he is able to subdue all things unto himself". This is our "blessed hope". We have referred to it here, and not in the order in which it stands in this chapter, in order to show what it is that lies between the two—the beginning and the end of our Christian course. What is it that is to fill the place between these two? What is to occupy our hearts from the moment when we were in Christ, who is our life, to the moment when we shall be like Christ, who shall be our glory? What is the one object that is to ever fill our hearts and occupy our minds?

"That I May Know Him."

This is henceforth the Christian's great object. Nothing but this aim to get to know Christ (for this is the word used here, in Philippians 3:10). As verse 9 contained the explanation of the words "found in Him," so this verse (10) contains the explanation of how and why we are to get to know Christ.

We are henceforth no longer to know Him after the flesh, but to get to know Him as risen; the head of the New Creation in resurrection (II Corinthians 5:16,17). For this is how this knowledge is explained: "that I may get to know him and the power of his resurrection". Not to know merely the historical fact of his resurrection, but the "power" of it: *i.e.*, what its wondrous power has done for us. But how can we get to know this "power"? Ah! only by experiencing "the fellowship of

His sufferings": by learning that when He, the Head of the Body, suffered, all the members of that Body suffered in mysterious and blessed "fellowship with Him". Thus shall we get to know how we were "made conformable to Him in His death". Only when we have thus learned that we suffered when He suffered, and died when He died, can we begin to learn how we have risen also with Christ; and "get to know the power of His resurrection".

How few of us know what this "power" is, as it takes us out of the old creation and sets us in the new creation, where "all things are of God" (II Corinthians 5:17). This then is our object, to get to know all that Christ is made unto us in resurrection power. How startling must these words have been as they fell upon the ears of Greeks (for this is the first city Paul set his foot in Europe). They had been brought up on the great motto of Solon, the wisest of the seven wise men of Greece. His motto was supposed by them to embody in itself the essence of all wisdom; and it consisted of only two words, which were carved over the entrance to the schools and colleges of Greece:

"Know Thyself."

But yet, how foolish are those words. For how can one know anything of himself by considering himself? If he looks at others, then he can see how different he is from them; and how much better or worse he may be than they. But it is only when we compare ourself with Christ, who is the wisdom and glory of God, that we learn what we really are; and how far short we come of that glory (Romans 3:23). It is only as we see ourselves in "the Balance of the Sanctuary," or by the side of the plumb-line of that Perfection, that we see, and get to know, our absolutely lost and ruined condition. Hence this new motto was thundered from heaven into the ears of those who sought to know themselves—

"That I may get to know Him."

Yes; this is our one object. This it is that will have the mighty transforming power over our lives. Every moment spent in seeking to know ourselves is a moment lost: and not only lost, but used to keep us from the one thing that alone can accomplish our object and teach us ourselves. Trying to know ourselves, we not only fail in the attempt, but we cease to learn Christ, which alone teaches us to know ourselves.

And yet, how many are spending their lives in this vain search? Running hither and thither to hear this man and that man. And, being constantly directed to this self-occupation, self- surrender, and self-examination, they are only led into trouble; or, into a joy which lasts only while the excitement is kept up.

Oh! to be occupied with Christ; to have Him for our object; and His resurrection power for our lives. This we shall have; and have increasingly as we get to know Christ. Again. What was it that led the heathen world into all its darkness, corruption, and sin? Just this: "they did not like to retain God in their knowledge. Professing themselves to be wise, they became fools, and changed the glory of the incorruptible God into the likeness of corruptible man" (Romans 1:22,28).

Like people to-day who, ignorant of God as He has revealed Himself in His Word, make their god, some with their own hands, or out of their own heads, vainly imagining He is what they think He is, and worshipping, like the heathen, "the unknown God," such an one as themselves. What was it that led Israel astray and brought upon them all their sorrows and sufferings? Isaiah opens with the Divine indictment, which gathers up in the briefest form the one great cause which lay at the root of all: "The ox knoweth his owner, And the ass his master's crib; But Israel doth not know, My People doth not consider."

See how the Lord Jesus confirms this in Luke 19:42-44, as He weeps over Jerusalem. All is summed up in the opening and closing words:

"If thou hadst known! even thou, at least in this thy day, the things that belong unto thy peace."

And then, turning to the reason for that judgment He adds: "Because thou knewest not the day of thy visitation."

And what is to be the acme of Israel's glory in the day of her restoration? Ah! then it shall come to pass that "they shall no more teach every man his neighbour saying, Know the Lord: for they shall all know me, from the least of them unto the greatest of them, saith the Lord" (Jeremiah 31:34). And what shall be Creation's glory; and the peace and joy of the whole earth? This sums up all:

"The earth shall be full of the knowledge of God, As the waters cover the sea" (Isaiah 11:9).

And what is the secret of our being able to glory only in the Lord, and to enjoy His blessing in this the day of our visitation? It is given in Jeremiah 9:23,24:

> *"Let not the wise man glory in his wisdom,*
> *Neither let the mighty man glory in his might,*
> *Let not the rich man glory in his riches:*
> *But let him that glorieth, glory in this,*
> ***that he understandeth and knoweth Me."***

We are thus brought round, and brought back to the one great duty, which should henceforth absorb our hearts and minds, and fill our days and years; viz., to be instant in our study of the Word of God, which is given to us with the one great, express, commanding purpose—the revelation of Himself, in order that we may

Get to Know Him.

They Sang His Praise. They Soon Forgat His Works

"Then believed they His words: they sang His praise. They soon forgat His works: they waited not for His counsel" (Psalm 106:12,13)

These are solemn words, because they record a solemn fact. They are true, not only of Israel but of God's people in all ages. They refer to that tendency in the heart of each one of us to cry unto the Lord in our trouble, and then to need the exhortation, "Oh that men would praise the Lord for His goodness" (Psalm 107:8), and even to sing His praise and then forget His works.

When God separated a people to Himself, it was not merely that He might be the God of Israel, but a God to Israel. He will not only have the people for Himself, but He will be their God, and "Happy is that people whose God is the Lord" (Psalm 144:15). This Psalm records many examples of the statement made in the text. The first refers to the deliverance from Egypt. For a brief moment we see them in the attitude of faith: "Then believed they His word, they sang His praise" (verse 12). They are on the wilderness side of the Red Sea—"THEN." The waters that opened just now for their salvation and closed again for the destruction of their enemies roll between them and the house of their bondage. They are celebrating in their song the triumphs of God's right hand. They measure everything by it. Not only do they sing of what it has done, but by faith they celebrate victories yet to come, Exodus 15. Compare verses 12 and 13 with 15-18, and note the repeated "shall," "shall," "shalt."

Not one thing remains to be done; all is accomplished to Faith. Faith is seen thus to be the substance of things hoped for, the evidence of things not seen. And now Moses and the children of Israel are silent, and Miriam and the women are taking up the strain, but still the burden is the same (verse 21). But what is the Divine comment on the scene? "They sang His praise, they soon forgat His works." So quickly does praise give place to murmurings: "And the whole congregation of the children of Israel murmured against Moses and Aaron in the wilderness (Exodus 16:2).

Is, then, the Lord's arm shortened that it cannot save? Is His ear that heard their cry in Egypt grown heavy that it cannot hear? No! But the instrument of deliverance has been leaned on instead of the Deliverer. Yes! So really is this true that as soon as Moses is out of sight, they run with haste to Aaron, and say: "Up, make us gods which shall go before us, for as for this Moses, the man that brought us up out of the land of Egypt, we know not what is become of him" (Exodus 32:1). The comment of the Spirit is: "They forgat God their Saviour which had done great things in Egypt"! (Psalm 106:21). And so it is ever! Where there is not a living God- wrought faith, man must have something to look to that is visible and tangible—that is IDOLATRY.Occupied with the instrument

We have another example of this in the days of the Judges. The people had gone into open idolatry, and the Lord had sold them into the hands of their enemies Yet (as in Psalm 106:8, 41- 44) "Nevertheless the Lord raised up judges which delivered them" (Judges 2:16). But there was man's "nevertheless" in verse 19; they returned to their evil ways after God's merciful deliverances, and in chapter 6 we see them greatly impoverished The hand of Midian prevails; the Midianites were as grasshoppers for multitude, the people betook themselves to mountains, dens, and caves, the highways were unoccupied, the harvest was reaped by others, there is no sustenance left for Israel. Then the Lord raised up Gideon, He looked on him and strengthened him; He went forth with him, and delivered Israel with a great deliverance by "the sword of the Lord and of Gideon." But Israel was occupied with the Instrument! and they say to Gideon: "Rule thou over us, both thou and thy son and thy son's son also: for thou hast delivered us from the hand of Midian" (Judges 8:22). It was "thou, thou." Gideon was true to God here, but a few verses later we find him making an ephod of the gold that had been given him, and "all Israel went a whoring after it, and it became a snare to Gideon and his house."

Again, if we turn from the times of the wilderness and the days of the Judges to the reigns of the Kings, it is still the same. The history of the Kings is a dreary record of provoking the Holy One of Israel to anger, so that but a few reigns, like those of Jehoshaphat, Hezekiah, and Josiah stand out as bright exceptions. Manasseh, indeed, did repent and reform at the end of his reign, but we read of his son Amon that "he did evil in the sight of the Lord as did Manasseh his father... and humbled not himself before the Lord as Manasseh his father had humbled himself, but Amon trespassed more and more." We see the condition of things worse and worse till Baal- worship was carried on in the Temple of Jehovah, and actually the horses of the idol were stabled in the house of the Lord (II Kings 23). At this juncture Amon's son Josiah succeeded to the throne, and the history of his reign is minutely given in II Chronicles 34 and 35.

"While he was yet young," he sought the Lord (II Chronicles 34:3), and four years afterward he set about purging the city and the land, and thus fulfilled a prophecy uttered 300 years before: "There came a man of God out of Judah by the word of the Lord unto Bethel: and Jeroboam stood by the altar to burn incense, and he cried against the altar in the word of the Lord, and said, 'O altar, altar! thus saith the Lord, behold a child shall be born unto the house of David, Josiah by name; and upon thee shall he offer the priests of the high places that burn incense upon thee, and men's bones shall be burnt upon thee" (I Kings 13:1,2). And although the messenger, the instrument employed, failed directly after delivering his message, yet the word of God could not fail. That word came to pass. The king, "Josiah by name," received a great encouragement for his work, and a solemn warning to "take heed" to the voice of the Lord, for in the midst of his labours "the Book of the Law" was found (II Chronicles 34:14). The king received it in its power, for he traced all the misery up to neglect of this blessed book (verses 19- 21). He learned that the Law may be neglected, though it cannot be broken. A blessed season from the Lord was vouchsafed, and the chapter which gives the record ends with the words: "All his days they departed not from following the Lord." Ah! "all his days"! Man's "nevertheless"

Yes, it is the same lesson still; the Lord Himself detects it, He sees the heart, and He has recorded what He saw in Jeremiah 3:6,10. Treacherous Judah "hath not turned unto Me with her whole heart, but feignedly, saith the Lord." Hence we read: "After all this... Necho King of Egypt came up to fight against Carchemish... and Josiah went out against him" (II Chronicles 35:20). Listen to Necho's words: "What have I to do with thee, thou King of Judah?. I come not against thee this day, but against the house wherewith I have war, for God commanded me to make haste; forbear thee from meddling with God who is with me that He destroy thee not" (verse 21).

Hark what the Scripture says: "Nevertheless Josiah would not turn his face from him... and hearkened not unto the words of Necho from the mouth of God" (verse 22), with fatal result. Oh, how solemn! how instructive! We are not told all the reasons, and how far, like Uzziah, "he was marvellously helped till he was strong. But when he was strong his heart was lifted up to his destruction" (II Chronicles 2:15,16). Like ungodly Ahab he disguised himself in the battle, but no disguise will hide us from God's eye, no shelter will avail us, and like another Ahab he is struck down by an arrow.

Sad! Solemn! and instructive lesson! Yet he was taken away from evil to come, and great lamentation was made for him (II Chronicles 35:25). Let us draw near and listen to the mourners. "The breath of our nostrils, the anointed of the Lord, was taken in their pits, of whom we said, 'Under His shadow we shall live among the heathen'" (Lamentations 4:20). Ah, it is the same lesson still. Israel served God "all his days," but at heart they were the "same generation." In the light of Josiah they walked, and not "in the light of the Lord." Upon "the breath of his nostrils "they lived, not on the words which proceeded out of the mouth of God. Under the shadow of Josiah they thought to dwell, and not under the shadow of the Almighty. These things happened of old, they are "written for our admonition." Like a bell swinging to and fro over the sunken rock, giving warning to the mariner, that hard by where he is passing others have made shipwreck, they sound in our ears: "Take heed, lest there be in any of you an evil heart of unbelief in departing from the living God."

The Christian life

No one is really a Christian, but he who has received the Word of God "with the Holy Ghost and with power." He who has done this has turned to God from every idol, and is entitled to know that the blood of Christ has cleansed from all sin; and in Him who is now at the right hand of God he has been brought nigh. But the Christian life down here is not merely a fresh direction given to religious instincts or to the fleshly activities of man. It is not the holding of certain views or the taking of certain vows; pledges, or badges, or the shaping the conduct after a certain course, but it is the having to do with God in Christ, believing God, obeying God, fearing God, walking with God, worshipping God, serving God, joying in God. In short, "setting the Lord always before us," and setting the heart and conscience before Him. All ministry of the Word is for this end, and is healthful only as it subserves it.

The days in which we live are marked by the same character as of old: "They sang His praise, they soon forgat His works." God is forgotten, the instrument is too much thought of; man is glorified, the creature is exalted as though the saint has anything which he has not received. See what godly jealousy was manifested, by that faithful pastor, Saint Paul: "Let no man glory in men" (I Corinthians 3:21). "These things, brethren, I have in a figure transferred to myself and Apollos... that ye might learn in us not to think of men above that which is written, that no one of you be puffed up for one against another" (I Corinthians 4:6). "The Lord gave... God giveth" (I Corinthians 3:5,7).

To lean on the instrument is the very essence of idolatry, for it displaces God. It is natural for us to do so because it is ever irksome to the flesh to be directly, continually, and absolutely depending upon God. When the stripling David returned from the fight, the women sang his praises (I Samuel 18:7); but they were no true daughters of Miriam, their song was not "The Lord hath triumphed gloriously, "but "Saul hath slain his thousands, and David his ten thousands"; and we read that "Saul eyed David from that day forward" (I Samuel 18:9).

While we may see in this Saul's envy and jealousy, we must note that it became David's "thorn in the flesh," the Divine antidote for man's praise, and though a "messenger of Satan," it ministered the love of God. There is but ONE on whom we may safely depend, only ONE under whose "shadow" we may dare to dwell. Of that One, the voice from the excellent glory has testified as the cloud hid Moses and Elias: "HEAR HIM" (Luke 9:33-35). What do we know of all this? Are we dwelling under His shadow, occupied with Him? Or are we taken up with instrumentalities, doctrines, observances, ceremonies, things about Christ instead of with Christ? Oh, to be occupied with Christ Himself! May God bless His Word to our hearts, reveal Christ to us in it, and open our ears to HEAR HIM!

The One Great Subject of the Word

The one great subject which runs through the whole Word of God is Christ: the promised seed of the woman in Gen. 3:15. This verse marks the depth of the ruin into which man had descended in the Fall; and it becomes the foundation of the rest of the Bible.

All hope of restoration for man and for creation is centred in Christ; who in due time should be born into the world, should suffer and die; and, in resurrection, should become the Head of a new creation, and should finally crush the head of the Old Serpent, who had brought in all the ruin. Christ, therefore, the King, and the Kingdom which He should eventually set up, become the one great subject which occupies the whole of the Word of God. Hence, He is the key to the Divine revelation in the Word; and apart from Him it cannot be understood.

The contents of the Bible must therefore be seen and arranged with reference to Him. The counsels and purposes of God are all centered in Christ.

1. In the Old Testament we have the King and the Kingdom in Promise and Prophecy, Illustration and Type.

2. In the Four Gospels we have the King and the Kingdom presented and proclaimed by John the Baptizer, and by Christ Himself. And we see the Kingdom rejected, and the King crucified.

3. In the Acts of the Apostles we have the Transition from the Kingdom to the Church. The Kingdom is once again offered to Israel by Peter; again it is rejected, Stephen is stoned, and Peter imprisoned (ch. 12.). Then Paul, who had been already chosen and called (ch. 9.), is commissioned for His Ministry (ch. 13.), and on the final rejection of his testimony concerning the Kingdom, he pronounces for the third and last time the sentence of judicial blindness in Isaiah 6, and declares that "the salvation of God is sent to the Gentiles" (Acts 28:25-28). In his final communication to Hebrew believers it is written that while in God's counsels all things had been put under Christ's feet, "we see NOT YET all things put under Him " (Heb. 2:7-9). The Kingdom thenceforth is in abeyance.

4. In the Epistles we have the King exalted, and (while the Kingdom is in abeyance) made the Head over all things to the Church, during this present Interval; the Dispensation of the grace of God.

5. In the Apocalypse we have the Revelation of the King in judgment; and we see the Kingdom set up, the King enthroned in power and glory, the promise fulfilled, and prophecy ended.

We may exhibit the above to the eye in the following Structure:

The one Subject of the Word as a Whole.

A. The King and the Kingdom in Promise and Prophecy. (The Old Testament.)

    B. The King presented, proclaimed, and rejected. The Mysteries (or Secrets) of the Kingdom revealed. Matt. 13:11, 34, 35. (The Four Gospels.)

        C. Transitional (The Acts). The Kingdom again offered and rejected. The Mystery of the Church made known. The Kingdom in abeyance (Heb. 2:8).

    B. The King exalted and made Head over all things to the Church, "which is His body, the fullness of Him that filleth all in all " (Eph. 1:22, 23). The Great Mystery completed (The Epistles).

A. The King and the Kingdom unveiled. The King enthroned, and the Kingdom set up with Divine judgment, power, and glory (Rev. 19, 20). Promise and prophecy fulfilled (The Apocalypse).

Here the correspondence is seen between these five members.

In A and A we have the King and the Kingdom.

In B and B we have the King and the mysteries (or secrets) of the Kingdom (Matt. 13).

In C, the central member, we have the present Interval, while the King is absent, the Holy Spirit present, and the Kingdom in abeyance, and the mystery of the Church revealed (Eph. 3). From the Structure it will be seen that the great subject of the whole Book is one. From Gen. 3:15 to Rev. 22., "THE COMING ONE" fills our vision.

This teaches us that the Coming of Christ is no newly invented subject of some modern faddists or fanatics, or cranks; but that Christ's coming has always been the Hope of His people. In "the fullness of time" He came: but having been rejected and slain He rose from the dead, and ascended to Heaven. There He is "seated" and "henceforth expecting until His enemies shall be placed as a footstool for His feet " (Heb. 10:13). Hence, Christ, "the Coming One," is the one all-pervading subject of the Word of God as a whole.

He is the *pneuma* or life-giving spirit of the written Word, without which the latter is dead. "As the body without the *pneuma* is dead" (Jas. 2:26), so the written Word without the pneuma is dead also. Christ is that pneuma or spirit. This is the whole argument of II Cor. 3. This is why the Lord Jesus could say of the Scriptures: "They testify of ME" (John 1:45; 5:39; Luke 24:44, 45).

Their one great design is to tell of the Coming One. All else is subordinated to this. This is why we see the ordinary events in a household combining with the grandest visions of a prophet to testify of Him who fills all Scripture. It may be said of the written Word, as it is of the New Jerusalem, "The Lamb is the light thereof " (Rev. 21:23).

Apart from Him, the natural eye of man sees only outward historical details and circumstances; some in themselves appearing to him trifling, others offensive, and pursued at a length which seems disproportionate to the whole; while things which "angels desire to look into" are passed over in a few words, or in silence.

But once let "the spiritual mind" see Christ testified of "in Moses and all the prophets," then all assumes a new aspect: trifles that seem hardly worth recording fill the whole vision and light up the written Word and make it to shine with the glory of the Divine presence. Then we see why the Inspired writer dwells on a matter which to the outward eye seems trivial compared with other things which we may deem to be of world-wide importance. Then we observe in an event, seemingly casual and unimportant, something which tells forth the plans and counsels of God, by which He is shaping everything to His own ends. Nothing appears to us then either great or small. All is seen to be Divine when the Coming One is recognized as the one subject of the Word of God. This is the master-key of the Scriptures of truth.

"These are they that testify of ME." Bearing this key in our hand we can unlock the precious treasures of the Word; and understand words, and hints; apparently casual expressions, circumstances, and events, which in themselves, and apart from Him, are meaningless. It is the use of this master-key and this first great foundation principle which is to be observed in the study of the "Word" and "words" of God. It is when we, in every part, have found "HIM of whom Moses in the law, and the prophets, did write" (John 1:45), that we can understand those parts of Scripture which are "a stone of stumbling and a rock of offence" to many; that we can explain much that is otherwise difficult; see clearly much that before was obscure; answer objections that are brought against the Word; and "put to silence the ignorance of foolish men." The moment this master-key is used types will be seen foreshadowing the Coming King, and showing forth His sufferings and His Glory. Events and circumstances will show forth His wondrous deeds and tell of the coming glory of His kingdom.

A New Creation

Therefore if any man be in Christ, he is a new creature: old things are passed away; behold, all things are become new" (II Corinthians 5:17).

The Scriptures reveal to us many new things. In Isaiah 42:9, we read: "New things do I declare"; and God goes on to speak of the new song which is to be sung in view of His work for restored Israel. We read in Lamentations 3:22,23, "The Lord's mercies are new every morning." We read in Ezekiel 36:26, of "a new heart and a new spirit."

In the text before us we read of the new creature. We read in Ephesians 2:15, of "the one new man"; in Revelation 21 and 22, of "the new heavens and the new earth," also of "the new Jerusalem," and of a glorious time when it will be said, "Behold, I make all things new." Perhaps the most important of all these wondrous things is that which is spoken of in our text, because without this new creation, none of the other new things can be known or enjoyed. Having this, we have all the others.

The contrasts, old and new

Let us consider, first of all, the contrasts—Old and New. The Second Epistle to the Corinthians seems to be an Epistle of contrasts; it abounds in them from beginning to end. Led by the Holy Spirit, the Apostle Paul contrasts, in chapter 1:5, the sufferings which abound in the child of God with the consolations which abound in Christ. At the close of chapter 2, verse 16, we meet with a very solemn contrast, which is seen by the spiritual eye throughout the whole of God's Word. True, the carnal mind objects to, indeed hates, such contrasts between the living and the dead, between the regenerate and the unregenerate; but the Holy Spirit invariably marks these contrasts, and those who are taught by Him see them and love them (see verse 14). Note again, in verse 15, another contrast "We are unto God a sweet savour of Christ, in them that are saved, and in them that perish." It is we, not our testimony. The burden of the Word of the Lord showed the Apostle his insufficiency, while at the same time he knew that his sufficiency was of God.

The third chapter is full of contrasts; in verse 1 we have man's commendation and God's commendation; in verse 2 and 3, man's writing and the Spirit's writing; in verse 5, man's insufficiency and God's sufficiency; in verse 6 the letter and the spirit; in verses 7-9, condemnation and righteousness. The fourth chapter contains many wonderful contrasts and paradoxes; in verse 8, "We are troubled on every side, yet not distressed; we are perplexed, but not in despair." One may say, "Ah! that is not I"; but look at the margin, "But not altogether without help." Can we not say that? Verse 9: "Cast down, but not destroyed." We do fall, but not from grace, being upheld by "a Loving Omnipotent Hand." At the end of the chapter again we see wonderful contrasts; in verse 16, our outward man perishing, but our inward man renewed day by day; in verse 17 our present light affliction, our future weight of glory; in verse 18, temporal things and eternal things: things seen and things unseen.

Each of these leads us to the contemplation of the words of our text. In considering this vast and important subject, note:

1. The Connection

"Therefore" (Verse 17). This is the conclusion of the Spirit's argument, or of the truths He had declared for the instruction, the comfort, and the edification of the saints at Corinth, and through them to the Church of God in all succeeding generations. His conclusion is that all old things, even those of Divine appointment, having served their purpose and waxen old, must pass away for ever, as of no value whatever in comparison with the eternal work of the new creation in Christ Jesus. Note next:
2. The Character of those spoken of

"If any man be in Christ." Observe, [in the King James Version] there are words in italics which may be differently supplied thus: "If any man in Christ be made a new creature," or a new creation; the R.V. margin gives: "there is a new creation." Now creation is a Divine work, and therefore this excludes all means, all modes, all distinctions. Truth by the Holy Ghost is a great leveller. Turn to Galatians 3:28 and 6:15. The new creation does not consist in an acknowledgement of a form of sound words, or delight in a clear creed, or in prizing the outward so-called means of grace. It is ten thousand times more than these. The cross of Christ is God's monument erected over the grave of all carnal ordinances, all sensuous ceremonies, all fleshly sacrifices, all earthly types, all fleeting shadows. The cross of Christ is God's monument over the grave where He has buried all human distinctions, all human modes, all human means in matters pertaining to His creation work. IN CHRIST. This is a living union by the Spirit of God. It is not a mere profession of religion; it is not in self-condemnation but in Christ, justified and accepted (Ephesians 1:6). It is not in Adam dead, but in Christ alive (I Corinthians 15:22). In Christ by sovereign purpose; in Christ by sacred purchase; in Christ by spiritual power. Next look at:

3. The Condition

"A New Creation." What is it to create? Not to change, not to renovate, not to reform, not to improve, not the old nature adorned and beautified, not the flesh with its corruptions and lusts trimmed and trained; but it is the new and Divine nature imparted, with all its spiritual blessings and holy privileges. It is not the Old Adam made clean or religious, clothed and adorned. No! It is a something altogether NEW. Therefore, in Christ Jesus I am a partaker of the Divine nature; I am a partaker of His Resurrection-life, according to the Father's promise: "Eternal life, which God, that cannot lie, promised before the world began" (Titus 1:2).

Life was promised in Christ for His people before the world began; and in due time it is communicated to them through the ministry of the Word. How this is brought about, the poor child of God very often, knows not, and when questioned about it, he can only say, like the blind man in John 9:25: "One thing I know, that, whereas I was blind, now I see." Once I was blind and dead to God's Christ, God's covenant, God's salvation; I was dead to all interest in the precious atoning blood, to justifying righteousness, regenerating grace, and restoring mercy, also to that peace ,which passeth all understanding. But now, in living union with Christ, I love to dwell on those glorious verities which are found alone in Him and through Him. I love the company of those who delight in the Father's eternal love, the son's redeeming grace, and the Spirit's regenerating mercy.

A new Divine nature (II Peter 1:4) is not a mere influence, is not a mere passing religious feeling induced by ravishing music or pathetic story, but a real existence in living union with a crucified, risen, exalted, glorified, coming Lord. What a glorious union! One with the person of a glorified Christ! No words can describe it better than John 17:21-23: "That they all may be one; as Thou Father art in Me, and I in Thee; that they also may be one in Us, that the world may believe that Thou hast sent Me. And the glory which Thou gavest Me I have given them; that they may be one even as We are one. I in Thee, and Thou in Me, that they may be made perfect in one; and that the world may believe that Thou hast sent Me, and hast loved them as Thou hast loved Me" (John 17:22,23).

This is a glorious, marvellous, mysterious Oneness, which can never be understood until we stand perfect and complete in the light of His glory. Then we shall know even as we are known, for His Father is our Father; His righteousness is our righteousness; His nature is our nature; His home is our home; His glory is our glory.

4. The Deliverances Enjoyed

"Old things are passed away." What are these "old things? "

(1). Blessed be God, that old thing, SIN, which before I was in Christ manifested its power and maintained its authority over me, is gone—passed away. Do you ask, How did it pass away? I can answer you only in the words of Isaiah 53:6, "The Lord hath laid on Him the iniquity of us all"; and Hebrews 9:26, "Now once in the end of the world hath He appeared, to put away sin by the sacrifice of Himself."

(2). That old thing, THE CURSE OF THE LAW, has passed away. How? Read Galatians 3:13: "Christ hath redeemed us from the curse of the Law, being made a curse for us. for it is written 'Cursed is every one that hangeth on a tree.'" In thus becoming a curse for His people, He became "The end of the law for righteousness to every one that be-lieveth" (Romans 10:4). What expressive words! "The end of the law!" What does it mean? Why it means that He went to the end of all the Law's requirements, which He satisfied by the perfect obedience which He rendered to its precepts; that He went to the end of all the Law's penal threatenings which He silenced by the sufferings which He endured. What is the end of a debt? The payment! And Christ took over and paid every debt owed by His people, and thus ended it. Hence every transgression and even sin over which my chastened Spirit has grieved, is passed away !

(3). That old thing, CONDEMNATION. All that was due to me was borne by my sinless Surety, by Him who said, when they sought and found Him: "If ye seek Me, let these go their way" (John 18:8). Hence: "There is therefore now no condemnation to them which are in Christ Jesus" (Romans 8:1).

(4). That old thing, FEAR OF DEATH, is passed away, for "Jesus Christ... hath abolished death, and brought life and immortality to light by the Gospel" (II Timothy 1:10). Christ hath abolished death, and brought to light, and procured for us, life and immortality; and "When Christ, who is our Life shall appear, then shall ye also appear with Him in glory" (Colossians 3:4). Yes, old things have passed away. My old notions of salvation by merit; by co-operation—I doing something and Jesus Christ the rest—all such thoughts have passed away! My old, degrading views of Christ have passed away in the light of His Glorious Gospel, and I see Him "altogether lovely," His salvation perfect, His righteousness complete, His intercession all-prevailing, His glorious coming sure. He is the beginner and the finisher of faith, the performer of all things for me in the presence of His Father and mine. Look now at:

5. The Privileges Possessed

"Behold all things are become new." Yes, the man in Christ is a new man, with a new life in a new world. "All things are become new." He has life in Christ, he has immortality in Christ. He has life instead of death, salvation instead of sin, justification instead of condemnation, acceptance instead of banishment, peace instead of enmity. We have new affections, fixed upon things above; new hopes, entering within the veil; a new song put in our mouth; and a new heart with which to praise Him for setting our feet on the Rock of Ages, for ordering our goings, for holding our hand, for guiding our feet into the way of peace.

May it be ours to know the blessedness and power of these divinely "new things," and to go on our way rejoicing, while waiting for that great proclamation to go forth—"Behold I make all things new," and walking in newness of life, to the praise and glory of God.

"THE RESURRECTION OF THE BODY"

There are few subjects that are made more of in the word of God, and there are few subjects that are more set at nought by the traditions of men, than the doctrine of the Resurrection. I believe that it was the late Mr. Spurgeon who lamented the fact that our English theology, while it was rich in every department of Christian doctrine, does not contain a single satisfactory work upon it; and a reference to a bibliography of the subject, such as you find in Alger's Future State, will convince anyone of that fact—a fact as instructive as it is remarkable. We are all constantly confessing in our Creed, "I look for the resurrection of the dead". Do we look for it`? We are all as constantly confessing, "I believe the forgiveness of sins". Do we believe it? I think that the two may go together; and we may say of them that all the thousands who take the Christian name upon their lips know little about the forgiveness of sins, and look but little for the resurrection of the dead. It was with special reference to the resurrection that our blessed Lord said to His enemies, "Ye do err, not knowing the Scriptures, nor the power of God". And we err with regard to this subject of the transformation of His people, because we are ignorant of what the word of God has to say about it; and we are ignorant, upon the other hand, about all that flows from the knowledge of the forgiveness of sin, because we are ignorant of the blessed standing and privilege which He has given us. We separate ourselves from Christ; we separate this great doctrine from Christ; and hence it is that, while He holds out the blessed hope for troubled hearts, and says, "If I go away, I will come again and receive you unto Myself", and "I am coming to gather My saints, to raise them that are asleep, and to change them and those that are alive and remain", we reply practically, "No, Lord, Thou needst not come for me; I am going to die, and come to Thee".

While we may draw our own inferences from what the Scriptures state, we shall all agree that it is highly important that we should clothe those views in Scriptural terms, and that we should ask and answer how far it is that this popular saying hope of the Lord's coming again to fulfil His promise, to receive us to Himself; and how far it has practically blotted out the hope of resurrection and disestablished it from the place it occupies in the word of God, and disestablished it altogether from the Church's various hymn-books as a great object of hope. This error crept into the Church at a very early date. You remember how the apostle speaks to some in the 15th chapter of the lst Corinthians, who say that there is "no resurrection of the dead"; and in writing to Timothy he refers to Hymenaeus and Philetus, who had led away some from the faith by saying that "the resurrection is past already". It is remarkable, and it is instructive and worthy of all attention, that, though there is so little said about death in the New Testament, and nothing about it at any rate as a hope; and though there is so much said about the blessed hope of the transformation of His people at their resurrection, yet in the 6th of John, four times in a few verses, Jesus says, "This is the Father's will which hath sent Me, that of all which He hath given Me I should lose nothing, but should raise it up again at tire last day"; and again, "This is the will of Him that sent Me" (so that the words of Jesus really are the Father's will), ."that every one which seeth the Son, and believeth on Him, may have everlasting life"; and, more than that, "1 will raise him up at the last day". And again, "No man can come to Me, except the Father which hath sent Me draw him: and I will raise hire tip at the last day". And again, "Whoso eateth My flesh, and drinketh My blood, hath eternal life; and I will raise him up at the last day". (John 6:39, 40, 44, 54.)

The greatest comfort which the greatest Comforter that the world ever knew had to give to a sister who had been bereaved of a beloved brother was, "Thy brother shall rise again". All hope is bound up with this great subject: and, if our Theology has no place in it for this great hope, then the sooner we change it the better; for remember that this subject is one wholly of revelation. There is not a man on the face of the earth who can tell us anything whatever about it, except what he himself learns from the word of God. It is not therefore a question of human reasoning; it is not a question of the opinion of great or learned men; it is not a question of any system of doctrine or of philosophy; but it is purely a question of Divine revelation.

Our eyes see at every street corner at the present moment a placard advertising a book, Death and afterwards, by a poor mortal woman; and what can she tell us about it? What does she know about it, except the lies that she has been taught by demons and evil angels? True, even with the Word of God in our hands, we know only "in part"; but, thank God, a time is coming when we shall know in whole, when "that which is perfect is come".

The great fact of the resurrection of the dead was known all along the ages, and it was the hope of God's people; but a great secret was made known with regard to it by Jehovah to the Apostle Paul. Our Lord had previously given a hint of it when, coming down from the mountain of transfiguration (see the 9th chapter of Mark), he said that they should tell no man of the things they had seen until the Son of man were risen "from" the dead. The disciples would not have been puzzled if the Lord had spoken simply of resurrection. He had merely spoken of resurrection, when He told Martha that her brother should rise again. She said, "I know that he shall rise again". But here He spoke of a different thing. He said here, "Till the Son of man be risen FROM the dead", and it says that they kept that saying to themselves, questioning one with another what the rising FROM the dead should mean. The resurrection of the dead-of dead people-that they knew. As to this resurrection from among the dead, they wondered what it could mean. But the revelation was made to the Apostle Paul, and he writes in 1 Cor. 15:51, "Behold, I show you a mystery"; that is, "Behold, I tell you a secret. I am going to tell you something that has hitherto remained hidden and been kept secret", just as the secret with regard to the Church—the Body of Christ-had been kept. "Behold, I tell you a secret. We shall not all sleep." And the heathen world before, and the world to-day who are ignorant of this secret, say one to another, "Ali, there are many things that are uncertain, but there is one thing that is certain, we must all die!" Thank God, we know a secret about that. We shall not all die; but whether we are alive and remain, or whether we fall asleep, we know that we shall be changed and raised at His coming.

I ought to remark, in passing, that wherever the resurrection of the Lord Jesus Christ is spoken of, and wherever the resurrection of His people is spoken of, it is always with this preposition, "From among the dead". It is not always observed in the Authorized Version, but I believe that in the Revised it is uniformly rendered "from"; so that, in studying this subject for yourselves, if you take the Revised Version you will make no mistake about the true usage of the reference in this matter of the resurrection.

But now it is time for us to ask, "How are the dead raised up?" Of course, man has got his thoughts upon it, many thoughts; and of one thing we are perfectly sure, that we shall find that they are contrary to God's thoughts. We may summarize the whole of them in four great classes. We may call the first one the GERM theory. It is a very ancient theory. It is an ancient Jewish theory. At any rate, it is a theory of the Talmud. It was entertained by some of the Fathers, such as Tertullian and Gregory of Nyssa and Basil. They supposed that there is a bone, or a certain substance, in the human body which nothing can destroy, and they say the name of it is "luz". You may pulverize it in a mortar, but you cannot destroy it. You cannot dissolve it in acids, or in other substances, and nothing upon earth can destroy it; and that is the germ from which the resurrection body will be made.

Well, after all, that is only an hypothesis. There is no Scripture for that at any rate, and what saith Scripture? It distinctly says, "That which thou sowest is not quickened except it die"; but this germ never dies, and therefore it cannot be quickened. "It is sown a natural body; it is raised a spiritual body." "That which is born of the flesh [and this germ is flesh] is flesh." The seed which is spoken of by the Holy Ghost in 1 Corinthians xv. is only an illustration. I think we can hardly say that it is intended to be an exactly analogous identical process; but it is an illustration, just as when the Lord said with regard to Himself, "Except a corn of wheat fall into the ground and die [and that means to dissolve and to go to corruption] it abideth alone; but if it die it bringeth forth much fruit". He referred to His own body. His own body did not die in that sense. It saw no corruption. And therefore the "much fruit" which it has produced shows that this is only an illustration.

And then the second great class of ideas may be included under the term of the IDENTITY theory. This is a later theory, but it was an early Christian theory, and several of the Fathers professed it. Tatian and Tertullian and others believed that cripples would rise cripples, that infants would rise infants. Jerome believed that everyone would rise at about thirty years of age, at whatever age he died. Of course, that is only theory. The Mahometans hold this; and the mediaeval or scholastic Fathers held that as a person died so he would be raised. That is why, at this very moment, if a Mahometan is wounded in battle, he will never suffer his limb to be amputated. He would rather die in any agony, because he believes that he will rise again exactly as he dies. But this theory is met by such scriptures as these: "Thou sowest not that body that shall be"; "Flesh and blood cannot inherit the kingdom of God." We know that the earthly house of this tabernacle is to be dissolved, and that we are to have a new house, a house from heaven. These scriptures effectually dispose of what we may call the identity theory.

And then the third theory we may call the: RE-INCARNATION theory. That is the theory of the great ancient religions of the East. It is being revived to-day under the guise of theosophy. Re- incarnation is one of the cardinal features of theosophy, the teaching of evil angels at the present moment. Satan is getting a circulation for this lie now, in order to prepare for the moment when he is to re-incarnate the man of sin. And there are many Christian writers who verge very closely on this theory. Even Archbishop Whately did in his *Future State*. There is something akin to it in Bishop Westcott's writings and in Bishop Perowne's. They illustrate it thus, that it is all the same if the spirit inhabits another body; it is only another house. You may take this house down, and you may build another house with the same material, and it is practically the same house. But it is not the same thing. The body is a home for us, and if the house of our childhood were taken down and another house were built, we should go to it and should want to find the room where we found the Saviour. We should want to find the room where our mother died, or where some holy and hallowed scene took place. No; it says, "We are at home in the body"; and Job says, "I shall see Him for myself. Mine eyes shall behold Him, even though my reins be consumed within me". The Scriptures always assume that it is ourselves; and that has led to what we have called the identity theory.

You remember the words of the Lord Jesus which we have just repeated, "I will raise it up again", "I will raise him up again", four times in John vi. Then the apostle says to the Thessalonian saints, "I pray God your whole spirit and soul and body be preserved blameless unto the coming of our Lord Jesus Christ". "Who shall change our vile bodies"- the bodies of our humiliation, our humble bodies-"and make them like His own body of glory". "We shall be changed." We ourselves shall be changed. "He that raised up Christ from the dead shall also quicken your mortal bodies by His Spirit that dwelleth in you". The law of continuity is utterly broken down by this theory of re-incarnation.

And then, *fourthly*, there is what we may call the SPIRITUAL BODY theory. It is the Swedenborgian theory; it is the theory of the spiritualists, the teaching of demons. It is much more popular than you imagine. But this is also an ancient error, and it leads, as it did lead, to the denial of the resurrection altogether. According to this theory, resurrection practically takes place at death by a spiritual body which is evolved from the mortal body: but this utterly destroys resurrection as a hope; because the hope which is held out to us is, that those who are Christ's will be all raised together at His coming; not merely that we which are alive and remain are to be transformed together, but that those who are asleep are to be first raised, and then caught up together with the living ones to meet Him in the air. We are to be raised in a definite order-"Christ the firstfruits; afterward they that are Christ's at His coming". (1 Cor. 15:23, 24.) We are to be raised at a definite time, at the appearing of the Lord Jesus Christ; and that day is not the hour of each believer's death, but it is the hour of the Lord's appearing.

We are distinctly told by a direct revelation from the Lord, in 1 Thess. 4:15 (R.V.), "that we that are alive that are left unto the coming of the Lord, shall in no wise PRECEDE them that are fallen asleep". Why shall we not precede them, or get before them? Why! Because they are to be raised first; and then, when they are raised and changed, we shall be changed and caught up together with them in the clouds, to meet the Lord in the air. It cannot be that they have so preceded us! But this spiritual body theory utterly and entirely destroys this blessed hope of resurrection as a hope. It utterly reverses the teaching of Scripture as to death and as to judgment. It makes a mockery of those two great solemn statements, "Thou shall surely die", and, "There shall be no more death". And what utterly negatives this spiritual body theory is, that the resurrection body is to be like Christ's, and we know that His body was not such a body. His was a glorious body, and His body is the very type and the likeness and the illustration and the definition of what the raised bodies of the saints are to be. "We know", in spite of all these hypotheses and thoughts and imaginations, "that when He shall appear we shall be LIKE HIM".

How do we know it? Because God has told us that we shall be like Him. And What was He like? What was His resurrection body like? Well, as He came from the sepulchre the women held Him. So it was a body that could be held. He said to them, "Handle me, and see". So it was a body which could be handled, and a body which could be seen. lie said to Thomas, "Reach hither thy finger, and behold My hands: and reach hither thy hand, and thrust it into My side". So that it could be seen and handled and touched. The spear marks were visible, the prints of the nails must have been visible. And there is great meaning in those solemn words which refer to Israel, and yet await their fulfilment "They shall look upon Me whom they have pierced". We may imagine for a moment that solemn supper scene at Emmaus, when they knew not who He was; how when lie blessed the bread, and lifted up His hands in blessing, they may have seen the marks of the nails. He is the firstborn from the dead. He will have many brethren. It was by a resurrection of the dead that He was declared to be the Son of God. (Rom. 1:2.) And that is how ire shall be declared to be the sons of God. We have the blessed and high and holy privilege now; but it has to be "declared", it has to be "manifested", and we are told in Rom. 8:19 when that manifestation will take place. It will be when the body shall be redeemed from the grave, and the manifestation of the sons of Clod shall take place at the coming of our Lord Jesus Christ in the air. Resurrection was His right, because lie was Who He was. It is our blessed privilege and hope, because we are Whose we are.

Again we may ask, "How are the dead raised up?" And the answer to the question is, "By the power of God". Nicodemus asked, "How can these things be?" What was the answer? "God so loved the world, that He GAVE His only begotten Son". God's gift, therefore, was the answer to Nicodemus's "How?" And so in the next chapter, when the woman of Samaria asked, "How is it that Thou, being a Jew, askest drink of me, which am a woman of Samaria?" Jesus said, "If thou knewest the GIFT of God, and who it is that with to thee, Give Me to drink, thou wouldest have asked of Him, and He would have given thee living water". And so it is in 1 Cor. 15:35. "But some man will say", says the apostle, "How are the dead raised up, and with what body do they come?" What is the answer? "God GIVETH it a body as it hath pleased Him." The gift of God, the power of God as manifested in the gift of God, is the only answer to all our questions; and, thank God, we know this. "We know", as it says in 2 Cor. 5:1, "that if our earthly house of this tabernacle were dissolved". We know that "If it shall be dissolved". The particular Greek word for "if" there, with the mood of the verb that follows it, show that it is not at all a certainty. "If the house of our earthly tabernacle be dissolved." It is not at all certain that it will be. It may be. Of course, if we fall asleep in Jesus, it must be. But it may not be, because we may be "alive and remain" at His appearing. But, supposing that it should be dissolved, then we know that we blue a better one. We know that we have a house that God Himself shall build. We know that we have no longer an earthly house, but a heavenly one. And when shall we have it? Many commentators-in fact, all that I have looked at-say that we have this at death. But you notice that this chapter begins with the word "For"; and it is one in a series of reasons for a statement that has been previously made in the 14th verse of the 4th chapter: "Knowing that He which raised up the Lord Jesus shall raise up us also by Jesus, and shall present us with you".

How do we know it? By the next verse. "For all things", *etc.*; the next, "For which cause", *etc.*; the next, "For our light affliction", *etc.*; and then the verse of the next chapter, "For we know", *etc.* This is another of the reasons how it is that the Spirit which raised up the Lord Jesus shall raise us up and present us with Him. How? "For we know that if our earthly house of this tabernacle were dissolved, we have a building of God." And that is how we shall be raised up, and that is how we shall be presented. It is no mere transition, it is no mere evolution; but it is a transformation, it is a manifestation, it is a transfiguration, it is a resurrection, it is "the redemption of our body" (Rom. 8:23), it is the manifestation of our sonship. The Greek does not say "waiting for the adoption", but waiting for the sonship, waiting for the manifestation of our sonship in the resurrection of our bodies. So, while identity is not the word, CONTINUITY is the word, which really expresses the truth as to the transformation of God's people. The bodies that we possess at this moment are the same bodies in one sense as when we were children. We have photographs of ourselves, doubtless, at different ages-one taken in infancy, another in childhood, another in youth, and now those that have been recently taken. It is the same body, and yet philosophically and scientifically it is not the same. It is all the same for us, at any rate. "He that was dead came forth." Lazarus it was who came forth, and not another. "He that was dead sat up, and began to speak", and not another. "Women received their dead raised to life again", and they knew them and spoke to them. The grave, thank God, has already been robbed of some of its prey, and there are those who are to escape death altogether. The grave has been robbed of many, and death has been baffled by two; and, if we may answer this question, "How are the dead raised up"? in a definite statement, I would express it by the words CONTINUITY and re-creation: and that is why we are exhorted in 1 Peter iv. 19, "Wherefore let them that suffer according to the will of God commit the keeping of their souls to Him in well doing, as unto a faithful Creator". In fact, the transfiguration of the Lord Jesus Christ Himself is the type of the resurrection body, and that was a visible body. Moses and Elijah "appeared in glory", it says. But Christ's body was so glorious, and His raiment so white, "as no fuller on earth can white them". It was the glory of the revelation of the King. It is a specimen of the King coming in His kingdom with those who had been raised from the dead and those who had been changed.

But let us for a moment pay a visit, as Jeremiah did, to the potter's house, in Jeremiah 18:1-4. "The word which came to Jeremiah from the Lord, saying, Arise, and go down to the potter's house, and there I will cause thee to hear My words. Then I went down to the potter's house, and, behold, he wrought a work on the wheels. And the vessel that he made of clay was marred in the hand of the potter: so he made it again another vessel, as seemed good to the potter to make it." In the margin we read "he returned and made". If we look at the immediate context, we will find that the interpretation of these words refers to the house of Israel; but there is an application of the words that goes very much farther than their interpretation. The context shows that the interpretation belongs solely to the house of Israel; but we may apply the passage as exhibiting a great and divine principle which we see in all the works of God.

You see it, for example, in the COVENANT of works which He made with Israel. That was made, and man has always marred everything with which God has ever entrusted him. "Which My covenant they brake". The first covenant of works was like that vessel marred upon the wheels; and then He made another as seemed good to the potter to make it. And it is written of this covenant that if the first "had been faultless, then should no place have been sought for the second" (Heb. 8:7); but it was broken by His faulty people, and therefore a new covenant was made as it pleased the potter to make it.

And so it is with regard to THE EARTH. The earth was created in glory and beauty, but it has been marred. Sin entered, the curse was pronounced, and this earth has been marred in the hands of the potter. It is not going to be mended, but there is going to be a new one. "I saw a new heaven and a new earth: for the first heaven and the first earth were passed away." (Rev. 21:l.) And it was made "as it seemed good to the potter to make it".

It is true of our OLD NATURE that it has been marred in our first parents, and we know how it is marred in each one of us. It is never God's principle to mend that which man has marred. He always makes something new. And so He now makes a new creation in Christ Jesus. As the old nature is fallen and marred, man must have a new nature given to him. The new wine cannot be put into old wine skins, the new piece of cloth cannot be put upon the old garment; but the new wine must be put into new wine skins, and then both are preserved. And so with our bodies. These BODIES of humiliation, which are made of clay like the vessel of the potter, have been marred upon the wheel. As soon as we are born we begin to die. There are the seeds of suffering and disease and death in every one of us. We are made of clay, and marred upon the wheel. But the potter "returned" and made it again another vessel, as it seemed good to the potter to make it. And so with these transformed bodies at the resurrection, when the great potter Himself shall return. He will make them again another body, as it hath pleased Him: and so, whether it be the old nature, whether it be the heart, whether it he our bodies, they are never mended or repaired or improved or reformed; but they are condemned, and a new nature and a new heart is given, and by-and-by new bodies will be bestowed. Oh, what a depth of meaning there is in those few simple words-"He made it again another vessel, as seemed good to the potter to make it". "God giveth it a body as it hath pleased Him." (I Cor. 15:38.)

And so you find in Hebrews 10, with reference to the sacrifices and offerings which were under the first covenant, it is said they are all taken away because they were marred in their use; and then He said, "Lo, I come to do Thy will, O God". In each case "He taketh away the first, that he may establish the second". (Heb. 10:9.) Thank God, THE SECOND IS ALWAYS ESTABLISHED. And so it will be with these new glorious bodies. They will be established. These poor vile bodies will be soon taken away and disestablished; but that which is to come will be established for ever and ever in glory.

This is our hope, and you will see how it is all bound up in Christ. It shuts us up entirely to Him; but people do not heed it. The shepherds went and told the people about His first corning. It says, the people "wondered". That is all. The people wondered, and they went on talking about the topics of the day. The topics of the day were very much like the topics of our day-taxes, and commerce, and politics. Augustus had just made a taxing throughout the empire, and that was doubtless the great matter of conversation. They "wondered", and passed on with their business.

But the early Christians cherished this blessed hope, and the testimony of Gibbon is worth repeating. It is contained in a few words from the 15th chapter of his 1st volume. This great truth of the Lord's coming, and our being raised at His coming, was universally believed among these early Christians. He says, "The approach of this event had been predicted by the apostles. The tradition of it was preserved by their nearest disciples, and those who understood in their literal sense the discourses of Christ Himself were obliged to expect the coming of the Son of man before that generation was totally extinguished". [That is where Gibbon was wrong. They were not obliged to expect it before that generation was extinguished; but the fact remains that they did.] "As long as for wise purposes this error" [you see we have the testimony of an enemy who does not believe this truth himself] "as long as for wise purposes this error was permitted to subsist in the church, it was productive of the most salutary effect on the faith and practice of Christians". There is the testimony of an enemy then to this truth, as to the effect it produced upon the lives of those who held it. Oh, that Christians to-day would try this experiment! Oh, that we might be influenced by this blessed hope now! that we might accustom ourselves to looking for it, just as an army is practised in meeting a night attack, or just as upon a vessel the crew is practised by a false alarm of fire, so that each man may go to his right station. Oh that we might rehearse for ourselves, and practice for ourselves, the waiting for this assembling shoutthe waiting to hear the voice of the archangel and the trump of God! That will be an assembling shout. The trump of God is for the same purpose. See in Numbers x. 7, "When the congregation IS TO BE GATHERED TOGETHER, ye shall blow". And when His people are to be gathered together in the air this trump of God shall sound. But He says, "Ye shall not sound an alarm". No, it will be the signal for our being gathered together unto Him. It will not. be an alarm for us, but it will be a blessed assembling shout and gathering trump. As Christ is the blessed object and centre of our hope, so He is presented to us in this great subject. "He that bath this hope in Him"-not in himself. "He that hath this hope in Christ". What hope? Why the hope of being like Him at His appearing, when we shall see Him as He is. He that hath this hope fixed upon Him, what does he do? What is the effect of it? "Every one that hath this hope in Him purifieth himself, even as He is pure." Yes, it is a purifying hope. And why is the low standard of walk among Christians at the present day so much deplored? Why are so many efforts put forth for raising the standard of this walk? Because that standard has been changed. And why? Because this purifying hope is not held. Why are other methods tried and sought after for the promotion of purity of life, and this great divine advent method not tried? Here is God's method to secure our purity of life and walk. "He that hath this hope" (of the transformation of His people)-he that hath this blessed hope fixed upon him-"purifieth himself". And this Divine method cannot be carried too far. Other methods which men may propose to you may be carried too far. They are carried too far; but you will never carry this one too far. You can never look to Christ too much. You can never look for Christ too much. There will never be any ill effect from looking to Him; and, whatever may be left uncertain from the consideration of this subject, we may be sure that, with all our knowledge and all our thoughts about it, we shall surely say, when this blessed hope is realized, "The half was not told me". It will surely be beyond all that we have ever expected: it will surely exceed all that we ever desired: for "it doth not yet appear what we shall be: but we know that, when He shall appear, we shall be like Him; for we shall see Him as He is".

A Refreshing Study On The Resurrection

Scripture shuts us up to the blessed hope of being reunited in resurrection. That is why the death of believers is so often called "sleep"; and dying is called "falling asleep"; because of the assured hope of awakening in resurrection. It's language is, "David fell on sleep" (Acts 13:36), not David's body, or David's soul. "Stephen ... fell asleep" (Acts 7:60). "Lazarus sleepeth" (John 11:11), which is explained, when the Lord afterward speaks "plainly", as meaning "Lazarus is dead" (v. 14).

Now, when the Holy Spirit uses one thing to describe or explain another, He does not choose the opposite word or expression. If He speaks of night, He does not use the word light. If He speaks of daylight, He does not use the word night. He does not put "sweet for bitter, and bitter for sweet" (Isa. 5:20). He uses adultery to illustrate Idolatry; He does not use virtue. And so, if He uses the word "sleep" of death, it is because sleep illustrates to us what the condition of death is like. If Tradition be the truth, He ought to have used the word awake, or wakefulness. But the Lord first uses a Figure, and says "Lazarus sleepeth"; and afterwards, when He speaks "plainly" He says "Lazarus is dead". Why? Because sleep expresses and describes the condition of the "unclothed" state. In normal sleep, there is no consciousness. For the Lord, therefore, to have used this word "sleep" to represent the very opposite condition of conscious wakefulness, would have been indeed to mislead us. But all His words are perfect; and are used for the purpose of teaching us, and not for leading us astray.

So effectually has Satan's lie, "thou shalt not surely die", succeeded and accomplished its purpose that, though the Lord Jesus said "I will come again and receive you unto Myself", Christendom says, with one voice, "No! Lord. Thou needest not come for me: I will die and come to Thee". Thus the blessed hope of resurrection and the coming of the Lord have been well nigh blotted out from the belief of the Churches; and the promise of the Lord been made of none effect by the ravages of Tradition.

In Phil. 2:27, we read that Epaphraditus "was sick nigh unto death; but God had mercy on him"..So that it was mercy to preserve Epaphraditus from death. This could hardly be called "mercy" if death were the "gate of glory", according to popular tradition.

In 2 Cor. 1:10-11, it was deliverance of no ordinary kind when Paul himself was "delivered from so great a death" which called for corresponding greatness of thanksgiving for God's answer to their prayers on his behalf. Moreover, he trusted that God would still deliver him. It is clear from 2 Cor. 5:4 that Paul did not wish for death; for he distinctly says "not for that he would be unclothed, but clothed upon (*i.e.* in resurrection and "change") that mortality might be swallowed up of LIFE"; not of death. This is what he was so "earnestly desiring" (v.2)

Hezekiah also had reason to praise God for delivering him from "the king of terrors". It was "mercy" shown to Epaphraditus; it was "a gift" to Paul; it was "love" to Hezekiah. He says (Isa. 38:17- 19): "For the grave (Heb. *sheol*) cannot praise thee, death cannot celebrate thee: They that go down into the pit cannot hope for thy truth. The living, the living, he shall praise Thee, as I do this day."

On the other hand the death of Moses was permitted, for it was his punishment; therefore, there was no deliverance for him though he sought it (Deut. 1:37; 3:23,27; 4:21,22; 31:2). Surely it could have been no punishment if death is not death; but, as is universally held, the gate of paradise!

In 1 Thes. 4:15, we read: "This we say unto you by the Word of the Lord, that we which are alive and remain shall not precede them which are asleep."

To agree with Tradition this ought to have been written, "shall not precede them which are already with the Lord". But this would have made nonsense; and there is nothing of that in the Word of God.

While we may draw our own inferences from what the Scriptures state, we shall all agree that it is highly important that we should clothe these views in Scriptural terms, and that we should ask and answer how far it is that these popular sayings have practically, at any rate until recent years, blotted out the hope of resurrection, the hope of the Lord's coming again to fulfill His promise, to receive us to Himself. You remember how the apostle speaks to some in the 15th chapter of 1st Corinthians, who say that there is "no resurrection of the dead"; and in writing to Timothy he refers to Hymenaeus & Philetus, who had led some away from the faith by saying that "the resurrection is past already".

The greatest comfort which the greatest Comforter that the world ever knew had to give to a sister who had been bereaved of a beloved brother was, "Thy brother shall rise again." All hope is bound up with this great subject: and, if our Theology has no place in it for this great hope, then the sooner we change it the better; for remember that this subject is one of revelation.

We are expressly enjoined by the Lord Himself: "Marvel not at this: for the hour is coming in the which all that are in the graves shall hear His voice" (John 5:28). These are the Lord's own words, and they tell us where His Voice will be heard; and, that is not in heaven, not in Paradise, or in any so-called "intermediate state", but in "the GRAVES". With this agrees Dan. 12:2, which tells us that those who "awake" in resurrection will be those "that sleep in the dust of the earth"; from which man was "taken" (Gen. 2:7; 3:23), and to which he must return (Gen. 3:19; Eccl. 12:7). Psalm 146:4 declares of man, "His breath goes forth, He returneth to his earth; In that very day his thoughts perish." The passage says nothing about the "body". It is whatever has done the thinking. the "body" does not think. The "body", apart from the spirit, has no thoughts. Whatever has had the "thoughts" has them no more; and this is "man".

There is Eccl. 9:5, which declares that "The living know that they shall die; But the dead know not anything". It does not say dead bodies know not anything, but "the dead", i.e. dead people, who are set in contrast with the "living". As one of these "living", David says, by the Holy Spirit (Psa. 146:2; 104:33):"While I live will I praise the Lord: I will sing praises unto my God while I have any being". There would be no praising the Lord after he had ceased to "have any being". Why? Because "princes" and the "son of man" are helpless (Psa. 146:3,4). They return to their earth; and when they die, their "thoughts perish": and they "know not anything".

This is what God says about death. He explains it to us Himself. We need not therefore ask any man what it is. And if we did, his answer would be valueless, inasmuch as it is absolutely impossible for him to know anything of death, i.e. the death-state, beyond what God has told us in the Scriptures.

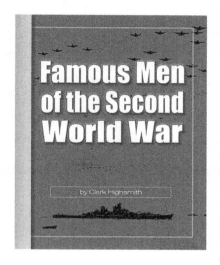

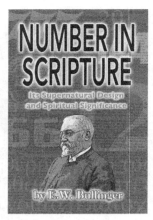
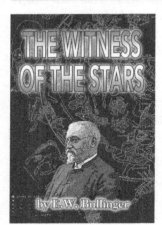

www.alacritypress.com
Other G.A. Henty Books by Alacrity Press

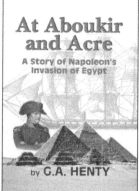

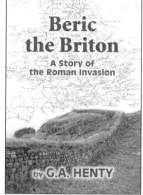

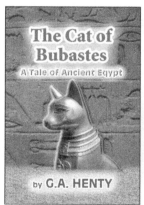

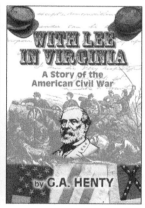

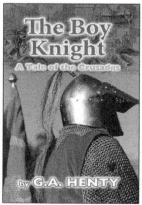

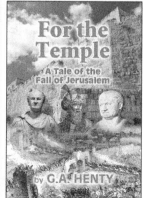

Made in the USA
Monee, IL
22 July 2024

62473481R00080